The Liturgical Environment:
WHAT THE DOCUMENTS SAY

Mark G. Boyer

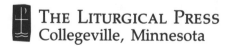
THE LITURGICAL PRESS
Collegeville, Minnesota

Cover design by Mark Coyle.

	2	3	4	5	6	7	8	9

Library of Congress Cataloging-in-Publication Data

Boyer, Mark G.
    The liturgical environment : what the documents say / Mark G.
Boyer.
        p. cm.
    Includes bibliographical references.
    ISBN 0-8146-1963-0
    1. Catholic Church—Liturgy. 2. Catholic Church—Liturgy—Papal
documents. 3. Churches (Canon law) I. Title.
BX1970.B6874 1990   90-19191
246'.9582—dc20   CIP

Dedicated to
my parents,
Jesse Lee Boyer and Verna Marie Boyer,
and my brothers and sisters,
Jane Marie Pashia,
Michael Jerome Boyer,
Diane Marie Maxwell,
Joseph Lee Boyer,
and Jeffrey Allen Boyer

Contents

Acknowledgments

Excerpts from the English translation of *Rite of Baptism for Children* © 1969, International Committee on English in the Liturgy, Inc. (ICEL); excerpts from the English translation of *The Roman Missal* © 1973, ICEL; excerpts from the English translation of *Rite of Penance* © 1974, ICEL; excerpts from the English translation of *Ordination of Deacons, Priests, and Bishops* © 1975, ICEL; excerpts from the *ICEL Newsletter* © 1977, ICEL; excerpts from the English translation of *Dedication of a Church and an Altar* © 1978, ICEL; excerpts from the English translation of *Pastoral Care of the Sick: Rites of Anointing and Viaticum* © 1982, ICEL; excerpts from the English translation of *Order of Christian Funerals* © 1985, ICEL; excerpts from the English translation of *Rite of Christian Initiation of Adults* © 1985, ICEL; and excerpts from the English translation of *Book of Blessings* © 1988, ICEL. All rights reserved.

Excerpts from *Environment and Art in Catholic Worship* © 1978 by the United States Catholic Conference (USCC), Washington, D.C.; *Liturgy Documentary Series 2: General Instruction of the Roman Missal* © 1982 USCC; *Music in Catholic Worship (revised edition)* © 1983 USCC; *This Holy and Living Sacrifice: Directory for the Celebration and Reception of Communion Under Both Kinds* © 1985 USCC; *Bishops' Committee on the Liturgy Newsletter Dec. 1974* © 1974 USCC; *May/June 1977* © 1977 USCC; *April/May 1978* © (C) 1978 USCC; *Feb. 1980* © 1980 USCC; *Nov. 1980* © 1980 USCC; *Dec. 1982* © 1982 USCC; *Nov. 1984* © 1984 USCC are used with permission. All rights reserved.

Canon 964 of the 1983 Code of Canon Law, © copyright by the Canon Law Society of America, 1983, Washington, DC 20064, is quoted with the permission of the copyright holder.

The quotation from John Allyn Melloh, "The Rite of Dedication," *Assembly* 10 (November 1983) is reprinted with permission of the Notre Dame Center for Pastoral Liturgy, University of Notre Dame, Notre Dame, Indiana.

The Constitution on the Sacred Liturgy (paragraphs 2, 5, 6, 7, 10, 11, 14, 19, 21, 26, 30, 35, 41, 42, 51, 55, 59, 61, 102, 106, 124); Dogmatic Constitution on the Church (paragraphs 7, 10, 11, 20); Decree on Concelebration and Communion Under Both Species (pages 57–60); Decree on the Ministry and Life of Priests (paragraph 2); On Holy Communion and the Worship of the Eucharistic Mystery Outside of Mass (paragraphs 2, 5, 6, 9, 11, 13, 82, 83, 94); Instruction on the Worship of the Eucharistic Mystery (introduction, paragraph 3, chapters 1, 2, 3) from *Vatican Council II: The Conciliar and Post Conciliar Documents*, Austin Flannery, ed. (Northport, N.Y.: Costello Publishing Co., 1975) are quoted with the permission of the copyright holder.

Photo Credits: Photos on pages 36, 59, 74, 88, 114, and 153 of St. Agnes Cathedral, diocese of Springfield-Cape Girardeau, Springfield, Missouri. Photo on page 129 of Holy Trinity Church, Springfield, Missouri. Photo on page 149 of St. Mary Church, Joplin, Missouri. Photos on pages 53 and 143 of author's personal collection of vessels and vestments.

Abbreviations

BCLN	*Bishops' Committee on the Liturgy Newsletter*
BB	*Book of Blessings*
CCL	*The Code of Canon Law: A Text and Commentary*
CIGI	"Christian Initiation, General Introduction," (found in RBC or RCIA)
CSL	The Constitution on the Sacred Liturgy
DCA	*Dedication of a Church and an Altar*
DCA:C	*The Dedication of a Church and an Altar: A Theological Commentary*
DCC	Dogmatic Constitution on the Church
DCCBS	Decree on Concelebration and Communion Under Both Species
DMLP	Decree on the Ministry and Life of Priests
EACW	*Environment and Art in Catholic Worship*
GIRM	General Instruction of the Roman Missal
HCWEM	"Holy Communion and Worship of the Eucharist Outside of Mass"
IWEM	"Instruction on the Worship of the Eucharistic Mystery"
LM	*Lectionary for Mass: Introduction*
MCW	*Music in Catholic Worship*
OCF	*Order of Christian Funerals*
PCPF	"Preparing and Celebrating the Paschal Feasts"
PCS	*Pastoral Care of the Sick: Rites of Anointing and Viaticum*
RBC	*Rite of Baptism for Children*
RCIA	*Rite of Christian Initiation of Adults*
RBOCC	"Rites of the Blessing of Oils and Consecrating the Chrism"

15

RP   *The Rite of Penance*

RP:OB   *The Roman Pontifical I,* "Ordination of a Bishop"

RP:OP   *The Roman Pontifical I,* "Ordination of Priests"

THLS   *This Holy and Living Sacrifice: Directory for the Celebration and Reception of Communion Under Both Kinds*

TS   *The Sacramentary*

Introduction

On December 4, 1963, the bishops of Vatican Council II issued The Constitution on the Sacred Liturgy. The emphasis of this document is the "full public worship" which "is performed by the Mystical Body of Jesus Christ, that is, by the Head and his members."[1] In fact, "in the restoration and promotion of the sacred liturgy the full and active participation by all the people is the aim to be considered before all else."[2]

The council Fathers state, "Mother Church earnestly desires that all the faithful should be led to that full, conscious, and active participation in liturgical celebrations which is demanded by the very nature of the liturgy, and to which the Christian people, 'a chosen race, a royal priesthood, a holy nation, a redeemed people' (1 Pet 2:9, 4–5) have a right and obligation by reason of their baptism."[3]

In order to accomplish participation in the liturgy, the council Fathers decreed that "both texts and rites should be drawn up so as to express more clearly the holy things which they signify. The Christian people, as far as is possible, should be able to understand them with ease and take part in them fully, actively, and as a community."[4] Furthermore, "to promote active participation, the people should be encouraged to take part by means of acclamations, responses, psalms, antiphons, hymns, as well as by actions, gestures and bodily attitudes. And at the proper time a reverent silence should be observed."[5]

Pastors are exhorted "to ensure that the faithful take part fully aware of what they are doing, actively engaged in the rite and enriched by it."[6] This is to be accomplished by promoting "the liturgical instruction of the faithful and also their active participation, both internal and external."[7]

The Fathers of Vatican II believe that "it is the liturgy through which, especially in the divine sacrifice of the Eucharist, 'the work of our redemption is accomplished,' and it is through the liturgy, especially, that the faith-

17

ful are enabled to express in their lives and manifest to others the mystery of Christ and the real nature of the true Church."[8]

Also, "the liturgy daily builds up those who are in the Church, making of them a holy temple of the Lord, a dwelling-place for God in the Spirit."[9] "The liturgy of the sacraments . . . sanctifies almost every event of their lives with the divine grace which flows from the paschal mystery of the Passion, Death and Resurrection of Christ. From this source all sacraments . . . draw their power."[10]

Because Jesus accomplished his task of redeeming humankind and giving perfect glory to God "principally by the paschal mystery of his blessed passion, resurrection from the dead, and glorious ascension, whereby 'dying he destroyed our death, and rising, restored our life,' "[11] "the Church celebrates the paschal mystery every seventh day, which day is appropriately called the Lord's Day or Sunday. For on this day Christ's faithful are bound to come together into one place. They should listen to the word of God and take part in the Eucharist, thus calling to mind the passion, resurrection, and glory of the Lord Jesus, and giving thanks to God who 'has begotten them again through the resurrection of Christ from the dead, unto a living hope' (1 Pet 1:3)."[12] The entire liturgical life revolves around the sacraments.[13]

The council Fathers conclude by declaring that "the liturgy is the summit toward which the activity of the Church is directed; it is also the fount from which all her power flows."[14]

The call for active participation by everyone in the liturgy is the norm that is applied throughout The Constitution on the Sacred Liturgy. Particularly, the norm is applied in the directive for the building of new churches: "Let great care be taken that they be suitable for the celebration of liturgical services and for the active participation of the faithful."[15]

It is within the environment of an ecclesial structure that the local Church gathers to celebrate the paschal mystery. Therefore, this structure must be illustrative of the norm of active participation. For, as The Constitution on the Sacred Liturgy states so clearly, "The principal manifestation of the Church consists in the full, active participation of all God's holy people in the same liturgical celebrations, especially in the same Eucharist, in one prayer, at one altar, at which the bishop presides, surrounded by his college of priests and by his ministers."[16]

The various documents that were issued in the wake of Vatican II attempt to enflesh the principle of active participation. The concern of this book is the theology of environment and the praxis, or practice, flowing from it, which should exemplify the principle of active participation. As many have learned over the course of the past years, "Good celebrations foster and nourish faith. Poor celebrations may weaken and destroy it."[17]

The ten chapters which follow are each divided into three sections. The first section presents the documents used in the study for the particular object (altar, ambo, etc.) under consideration along with their enfleshment of the active-participation principle.

The second section of each chapter details the post–Vatican II theology found in the documents. The praxis, which flows from the theology presented in the second section, is then considered in the third section of each chapter. The praxis should be an incarnation of the theology, which is itself founded on the active participation of the faithful.

It is hoped that this book will further the education of all persons involved in planning, building, decorating, and worshiping in a sacred environment.

Mark G. Boyer

Notes

1. CSL, no. 7.
2. Ibid., no. 14.
3. Ibid.
4. Ibid., no. 21.
5. Ibid., no. 30.
6. Ibid., no. 11.
7. Ibid., no. 19.
8. Ibid., no. 2.
9. Ibid.
10. Ibid., no. 61.
11. Ibid., no. 5.
12. Ibid., no. 106.
13. Cf. CSL, no. 6.
14. CSL, no. 10.
15. Ibid., no. 124.
16. Ibid., no. 41.
17. MCW, no. 6.

. . . The Church, in Christ,
is in the nature of sacrament—
a sign and instrument,
that is, of communion with God
and of unity among all. . . .

Dogmatic Constitution on the Church, no. 1

Chapter 1

Church: The Gathering of the Community

Ecclesial Documents

The norm of active participation is fleshed out in three ecclesial documents which deal with the building of a new church: (1) the rite of the *Dedication of a Church and an Altar,* (2) the General Instruction of the Roman Missal, and (3) *Environment and Art in Catholic Worship.*

The rite of the *Dedication of a Church and an Altar* places great emphasis on the participation of the people from the first instance. "The rite for the laying of a foundation stone or for beginning a new church" should be celebrated on a day "which would be convenient for the participation of the people."[1]

The introduction to the rite of "Laying of a Foundation Stone or Commencement of Work on the Building of a Church" stresses that "the parish priest (pastor) or others concerned should instruct [the people] in the meaning of the rite and the reverence to be shown towards the church which is to be built for them. It is also desirable that the people be asked to assist generously and willingly in the building of the church."[2] "Speaking equipment should be so arranged that the assembly may clearly hear the readings, prayer, and instructions."[3]

Once the building is completed, the church is to be dedicated. However, "in order that the people may take part fully in the rite of dedication, the rector of the church to be dedicated and others experienced in the pastoral ministry are to instruct them on the importance and value, spiritual, ecclesial, and missionary, of the celebration."[4]

"Accordingly, the people are to be instructed about the various parts of the church and their use, the rite of the dedication, and the chief liturgi-

21

cal symbols employed in it. Thus fully understanding the meaning of the dedication of a church through its rites and prayers, they may take an active, intelligent, and devout part in the sacred action."[5]

The General Instruction of the Roman Missal states: "Churches and other places of worship should . . . be suited to celebrating the liturgy and to ensuring the active participation of the faithful."[6] "The general plan of the sacred edifice should be such that in some way it conveys the image of the gathered assembly. It should also allow the participants to take the place most appropriate to them and assist all to carry out their individual functions properly. The congregation . . . should have a place that facilitates their active participation."[7]

Environment and Art in Catholic Worship, issued by the National Conference of Catholic Bishops with "the force of particular law in the dioceses of the United States,"[8] declares that "as common prayer and ecclesial experience, liturgy flourishes in a climate of hospitality: . . . a space in which people are seated together . . . in view of one another as well as the focal points of the rite, involved as participants and *not* as spectators."[9]

In another paragraph this document states: "The entire congregation is an active component. There is no audience, no passive element in the liturgical celebration."[10] "The assembly's celebration, that is, celebration in the midst of the faith community, by the whole community, is the normal and normative way of celebrating any sacrament or other liturgy."[11]

The structure of the building which is named "church" must foster this active participation because "the most powerful experience of the sacred is found in the celebration and the persons celebrating, that is, it is found in the action of the assembly: the living words, the living gestures, the living sacrifice, the living meal."[12]

With the general norm of active participation firmly established by these documents, each of the individual appointments necessary for celebration is then discussed. Our consideration here is the theology of the ecclesial structure found in the documents and the praxis which should flow from this theology. Therefore, after exploring the theology of the Church as presented by Vatican Council II, the praxis, which either fosters or impedes active participation, will be examined.

Theology of the Building Named "Church"

When beginning to outline a theology of the building referred to as "church," the physical structure is usually the starting point. However, the post–Vatican II documents declare that "the norm for designing liturgical space is the assembly and its liturgies. The building or cover enclosing the architectural space is a shelter or 'skin' for a liturgical action."[13]

"Among the symbols with which liturgy deals, none is more important than . . . the assembly of believers. It is common to use the same name to speak of the building in which those persons worship, but that use is misleading. In the words of ancient Christians, the building used for worship is called *domus ecclesiae,* the house of the Church."[14]

The rite for the *Dedication of a Church and an Altar* reiterates this by stating that "from early times the name 'church' has . . . been given to the building in which the Christian community gathers to hear the word of God, to pray together, to celebrate the sacraments, and to participate in the eucharist."[15] "The structure built of stone [is] a visible sign of the living Church, God's building, which is formed of the people themselves."[16]

Throughout the rite for the *Dedication of a Church and an Altar,* the people are referred to as "the temple"[17] gathered together by Christ as a people to be his own.[18] "This holy people, unified through the unity of the Father, Son, and Holy Spirit, is the Church, that is, the temple of God built of living stones, where the Father is worshiped in spirit and in truth."[19] "Christ is the cornerstone of the Church, and the temple that is . . . built by the living Church of the community of believers [is] at once the house of God and the house of God's people."[20]

No Need for Physical Walls

It is to be noted that "a Church may come into being, exist without masonry walls. Christ is the reason for its existence and the Holy Spirit the well-spring of its life. Yet since the pilgrim Church on earth cannot exist outside the categories of space and time, it usually erects buildings of stone which are the visible counterparts of the invisible 'house of God' (1 Cor 3:9), the place where the faithful meet in their worship or in holy assembly."[21]

The walls of the physical building, because they are visible, stand "as a special sign of the pilgrim Church on earth" and reflect "the Church dwelling in heaven."[22] The "chosen people now journeying through life" are guided by the word of God and find security and peace in the Church until they "arrive safely at their eternal home."[23]

Also, the "church is the image on earth of [the] heavenly city, . . . the dwelling place of [the] godhead in all its fullness."[24] The Father has "established the Church as [his] holy city, founded on the apostles, with

Jesus Christ its cornerstone. In that holy city [he] will be all in all for end-less ages, and Christ will be its light for ever."[25]

Finally, the Church "is the very body of Christ."[26] Just as the Father "made the body of [his] Son born of the Virgin, a temple consecrated to [his] glory, the dwelling place of [his] godhead in all its fullness,"[27] now the Church, built "with chosen stones, enlivened by the Spirit, and ce-mented together by love,"[28] is the incarnation of Christ, the visible body of Christ on earth.

A theology of the structure named "church," then, begins with the people who form the Church. "The congregation, its liturgical action, the furniture and the other objects it needs for its liturgical action—these indicate the necessity of a space, a place, a hall, or a building for the liturgy."[29] The theology does not begin with the building and then attempt to fit the people into it; theology begins with the people and designs a building around them.

Rite of Dedication

The theology of the structure named "church" is best exemplified in the rite of the *Dedication of a Church and an Altar*. While "the celebration of the eucharist is the most important rite, and the only necessary one, for the dedication of a church,"[30] other rites are used to signify the importance of the structure and to continually highlight it, so that the "space acquires a sacredness from the sacred action of the faith community which uses it."[31]

The rite of the dedication of a church begins with the entrance into the church; this may take place in three ways depending on the circumstances of time and place.[32]

THE FIRST FORM: THE PROCESSION

The first form of the entrance consists of a procession from a nearby church, or other place where all assemble, to the church to be dedicated.[33] This is "the most complete expression of the rite":[34] "All of the local Church is gathered together because all of it, hierarchically structured with its diversity of ministers and functions, is the celebrant of the rite of dedication."[35] The local Ordinary presides over the dedication ceremony.

The assembly gathers in a nearby church so that just "as light comes from light (the symbolism of the lighting of the candles in the Easter Vigil), as faith generates faith (the rite of baptism), so does one community emerge from another. Symbolically, from a house of worship, a sign of the mother community arises another house of worship, the sign and place of a new ecclesial community.''[36]

The ecclesial sense is further highlighted by the greeting of the bishop: ''The grace and peace of God be with all of you in his holy Church.''[37] Then, in the address to the people, the bishop makes ''reference to the fundamental importance of celebrating the eucharist in the dedication of a church: 'we have come together to dedicate this church by offering within it the sacrifice of Christ.' ''[38]

He also refers to ''the celebration of God's word: 'to receive his word with faith' ''; recalls ''the baptismal font as the birthplace of Christian community: 'our fellowship born in the one font of baptism' ''; and refers ''to the eucharistic table as the place of spiritual nourishment for the community: 'and sustained at the one table of the Lord.' ''[39]

After addressing the people, the procession to the church to be dedicated begins. ''The crossbearer leads the procession; the ministers follow; then the deacons or priests with the relics of the saints, ministers, or the faithful accompanying them on either side with lighted torches; then the concelebrating priests; then the bishop with two deacons; and lastly, the congregation.''[40] As the procession makes its way to the church to be dedicated, Psalm 122 is sung with the antiphon, ''Let us go rejoicing to the house of the Lord.''[41]

The procession ''is both a real journey of the community towards its new church and a sign of the journey of the pilgrim Church on earth towards the heavenly Temple.''[42] It is to be noted that ''the Church on its journey follows the cross of Christ. Moreover, when the procession also involves the transferral of relics of martyrs or saints it is well to stress that, in so doing, the Church follows in the steps of its members who have given lofty witness to the following of Christ.''[43]

The hymn sung during the journey is ''a lyrical expression of the joy of the Israelite pilgrims coming close to Jerusalem.''[44] It ''becomes the hymn of the Church which, though it has already realized within itself the mystery of the City of Zion, continues its journey towards the heavenly Jerusalem with the aid of signs, including that of the house of the Church.''[45]

Upon reaching the doors of the church to be dedicated, the procession comes to a halt.

> Representatives of those who have been involved in the building of the church (members of the parish or of the diocese, contributors, architects, workers)

hand over the building to the bishop, offering him according to place and circumstances either the legal documents for possession of the building, or the keys, or the plan of the building, or the book in which the progress of the work is described and the names of those in charge of it and the names of the workers recorded. One of the representatives addresses the bishop and the community in a few words, pointing out, if need be, what the new church expresses in its art and in its own special design.[46]

This part of the rite is designed to cover two distinct instances. "In one case the church arises out of community demands and faith, the result of collective participation: the members of a community put economic goods, intelligence, and labor at the service of the building of a house of prayer. In another instance, the participation of the community is very tenuous and indirect: the church is built at the instance of the state, which provides a sum of money and assigns the work to a corporation concerned almost exclusively with questions of profit and loss."[47]

Whatever the case, this part of the rite "will express the appreciation of the Church for labor, the hard work and fatigue that are a necessary part of building a church."[48] Furthermore, the new ecclesial edifice is presented to the bishop, who is the head of the diocesan Church.[49]

The signs used in the presentation "function . . . to highlight one aspect or another of the building's construction: juridical signs (a sign of ownership of the building or the keys); technical signs (the architectural drawings of the church); affective signs (an account of the construction with the signatures of administrators and workers)."[50]

Because "contemporary architecture, with its many contrasting trends, and in spite of uneven results, . . . seeks to express through new techniques, technology, and materials its own vision of the Church,"[51] the rite permits a representative of the community to point out what the new church expresses in its art and its design. "The history of sacred architecture documents instances in which the Church has wonderfully expressed the fullness of its mission or vocation: the sign of the presence of an ecclesial community, a quasi sacrament in which the blessed vision of the heavenly Jerusalem appears filtered through the veil of matter."[52]

After this brief address "the bishop then calls upon the priest to whom the pastoral care of the church has been entrusted to open the door."[53] "The door is closed because the church has not yet been inaugurated or 'open' to the celebration of the holy mysteries. It is opened so that entering through it the local Church might take possession of the new edifice."[54]

It is the priest, the "pastor of that part of the flock of Christ" who must not only "be the one who opens the door," but he must "also [be] the door."[55] The sheep, the assembly, then follow the chief shepherd, the bishop, and the local shepherd, the pastor, into the new building at the bishop's invitation: "Go within his gates giving thanks, enter his courts with songs of praise."[56]

The "invitation to cross the threshold of the new church . . . is taken from Psalm 99, which was sung by Israelite pilgrims as they entered the Temple on solemn liturgical feasts."[57]

As "the holy people begins its journey anew," Psalm 24 is sung with the antiphon "Lift high the ancient portals. The King of glory enters."[58] "The psalm is seen to have elements of a coronation: it proclaims that Christ, true King of Glory, is Lord and Head of the community of believers—the Church—which gathers him into itself. And this lordship of Christ over the Church-people has its symbolic expression in the solemn entry of the cross into the church-edifice where it will preside, glorious and peace-bringing, from the apse or altar, over the assembly."[59]

When a church is to be dedicated that has already been in general use for sacred celebrations, "the rite of opening the doors of the church is omitted, since the church is already open to the community."[60] Clearly, this directive reflects the norm of the general restoration of the liturgy that "both texts and rites . . . be drawn up so as to express more clearly the holy things which they signify" so that "the Christian people . . . be able to understand them with ease and take part in them fully, actively, and as a community."[61]

After entering the church, the bishop goes to the chair. The inauguration of a new presidential chair is treated in Chapter 4, "The Presidential Chair." The rite of blessing and sprinkling of water then takes place. This rite along with the rites for dedicating the altar and celebrating the Eucharist for the first time in the new church are covered in Chapter 2, "The Altar Is Christ." The Liturgy of the Word is treated in Chapter 3, "The Table of the Word of God," and the inauguration of the Blessed Sacrament chapel is covered in Chapter 6, "The Tabernacle and Eucharistic Reservation."

THE SECOND FORM: SOLEMN ENTRANCE

When the procession from one church or other place to the church to be dedicated cannot take place, "the people assemble at the door of the church to be dedicated."[62] There they are met by the bishop and his ministers. The greeting, address, and presentation of those who have been involved in the building of the church, the unlocking of the door of the church, and the procession into the new edifice take place as outlined above.[63]

THE THIRD FORM: SIMPLE ENTRANCE

The simple entrance is used when the solemn entrance or the procession cannot be employed. "The congregation assembles in the church itself."[64] The bishop and his ministers proceed "from the sacristy through the main body of the church to the sanctuary."[65] The greeting, address, and presentation of those who have been involved in the building of the church takes place as outlined above.[66]

Praxis

From this understanding of the theology of the structure of the building named "church," there flows a definite practice. As with all the revisions inaugurated by Vatican Council II, the theological background is given as a reason for the praxis which follows.

Titular Saint

Every church must have a titular saint. "Churches may have for their titular: the Blessed Trinity, our Lord Jesus Christ invoked according to a mystery of his life or a title already accepted in the sacred liturgy, the Holy Spirit, the Blessed Virgin Mary, likewise invoked according to some appellation already accepted in the sacred liturgy, one of the angels, or, finally, a saint inscribed in the Roman Martyrology or in an Appendix duly approved; but not a blessed, without an indult of the Apostolic See."[67]

Suitable Liturgical Space

The "church, as its nature requires, should be suitable for sacred celebrations. It should be dignified, evincing a noble beauty, not just costly display, and it should stand as a sign and symbol of heavenly things."[68]

Also, "the norm for designing liturgical space is the assembly and its liturgies."[69] "The *celebration* of the eucharist is the focus of the . . . assembly. As such, the major space of a church is designed for this *action*."[70] While "the people of God assembled at Mass possess an organic and hierarchical structure, expressed by the various ministries and action for each part of the celebration," they, at the same time, "form a complete and organic unity."[71]

"Special attention must be given to the unity of the entire liturgical space. . . . The space should communicate an integrity (a sense of one-ness, of wholeness) and a sense of being the gathering place of the initiated community. Within that one space there are different areas corresponding to different roles and functions, but the wholeness of the total space should be strikingly evident."[72] The aim of the liturgical space "is to facilitate the public worship and common prayer of the faith community."[73]

For this reason, "the general plan of the sacred edifice should be such that in some way it conveys the image of the gathered assembly," while being "clearly expressive of the unity of the entire holy people."[74] Particular attention, therefore, must be given to the altar, the ambo, the chair, the font, and the place for the reservation of the Eucharistic.[75]

Furniture

The objects used in ritual action, such as the altar, the ambo, the chair, the font, and the tabernacle, "are next in importance to the people them-selves and their total environment."[76] The design of the liturgical space must create "a feeling of contact with altar, ambo and celebrant's chair."[77] Furniture used in ritual action is "part of a total rite which everyone present should be able to experience as fully as possible."[78] The placement and use of such furniture "should allow for ease of movement."[79]

Visibility and Audibility

Two of the primary requirements which ensure participation by the to-tal assembly are visibility and audibility. Visibility is not interested only in the "mechanics of seeing,"[80] although this is important. Visibility also means that "a space must create a sense that what is seen is proximate, important and personal."[81] "The sense and variety of light, artificial or natural, [can] contribute greatly to what is seen."[82]

Visibility also implies eye contact. "Eye contact is important in any act of ministry—in reading, in preaching, in leading the congregation in music and prayer. Not only are the ministers to be visible to all present, but among themselves the faithful should be able to have visual contact."[83] It is im-portant that people are able to see the other members of the assembly with whom they are celebrating.

Like visibility, audibility entails more than simply hearing what is being said. With the aid of an amplifying system, one can hear at a great distance. However, this does not mean that a person is participating in the ritual action. "A space that does not require voice amplification is ideal. Where an amplifying system is necessary, provision for multiple microphone jacks should be made (e.g., at the altar, ambo, chair, font, space immediately in front of the congregation, and a few spots through the congregation)."[84]

Another consideration of audibility is the assembly's ability to hear itself. "The liturgical space must accommodate both speech and song."[85] Music, "sacred song united to words, . . . forms a necessary or integral part of the solemn liturgy. It imparts a sense of unity to the congregation and sets the appropriate tone for a particular celebration."[86] Therefore, the arrangement of benches or chairs for seating the assembly "should be so constructed and arranged that they maximize feelings of community and involvement. The arrangement should facilitate a clear view . . . of [the] members of the congregation."[87]

Visibility and audibility contribute to attentiveness, which is "part of one's share in the life of the community and something one owes the rest of the assembly."[88] This is the most important reason for designing a space and its seating so that "one can see the places of the ritual action" and "the faithful [are] . . . able to have visual contact, being attentive to one another as they celebrate the liturgy."[89]

Gesture, Posture, Procession

The sacred edifice must facilitate various gestures, postures, and processions because "the liturgy of the Church has been rich in a tradition of ritual movement" and "these actions . . . contribute to an environment which can foster prayer."[90]

Gestures, when done in common "contribute to the unity of the worshiping assembly. Gestures which are broad and full in both a visual and tactile sense, support the entire symbolic ritual. . . . They can . . . engage the entire assembly and bring them into an ever greater unity.[91]

Likewise, "it is important that the liturgical space can accommodate certain common postures: sitting for preparations, for listening, for silent reflection; standing for the gospel, solemn prayer, praise and acclamation; kneeling for adoration, penitential rites. Attentiveness, expressed in posture and eye contact, is a requirement for full participation and involvement in the liturgy."[92]

It is also important that worship spaces "allow for movement. Processions and interpretations through bodily movement (dance) can become meaningful parts of the liturgical celebration. . . . A procession should move from one place to another with some purpose (not simply around the same space), and should normally include the congregation. . . . The design of the space and arrangement of the seating should allow for this sort of movement."[93]

Genuineness

The guiding principle of praxis is genuineness. "The style in which a church is decorated should be a means to achieve noble simplicity. . . . The choice of materials for church appointments must be marked by concern for genuineness and by the intent to foster instruction of the faithful and the dignity of the place of worship."[94] "Every word, gesture, movement, object, appointment must be real in the sense that it is our own. It must come from the deepest understanding of ourselves (not careless, phony, counterfeit, pretentious, exaggerated, etc.)."[95]

Foyer

Before the various members of the assembly gather inside of the structure named "church" for liturgy, there is a previous gathering which takes place. "Planning for a convergence of pathways to the liturgical space in a concourse or foyer or other place adequate for gathering before or after liturgies is recommended. Such a gathering-space can encourage introductions, conversations, the sharing of refreshments after a liturgy, the building of the kind of community sense and feeling recognized now to be a prerequisite of good celebration."[96]

Other Facilities

Not only is it important to consider the assembly, the space, and the objects used in worship, but "proper planning of a church and its surroundings . . . requires attention . . . to those facilities for the comfort of the people that are usual in places of public gatherings."[97] This would include a place for parents with small children and for rest rooms.

Conclusion

In general, the reverence shown to the structure named "church" flows from the theology of the Church as found in the documents of the Church.

This theology of the Church should inform praxis. In other words, the theology of the Church should be seen in its incarnate form in the people, who are the Church, and in the building, in which they worship.

Notes

1. DCA, "Laying of a Foundation Stone or Commencement of Work on the Building of a Church," ch. 1, no. 2.

2. Ibid., no. 4.

3. Ibid., no. 7.

4. DCA, "Dedication of a Church," ch. 2, no. 20.

5. Ibid.

6. GIRM, no. 253.

7. Ibid., no. 257.

8. BCLN 21 (August–September 1985) 36.

9. EACW, no. 11.

10. Ibid., no. 30.

11. Ibid., no. 31.

12. Ibid., no. 29.

13. Ibid., no. 42.

14. Ibid., no. 28.

15. DCA, "Dedication of a Church," ch. 2, no. 1.

16. DCA, "Laying of a Foundation Stone or Commencement of Work on the Building of a Church," ch. 1, no. 1.

17. Ibid., nos. 13, 17, 30; cf. DCA, "Dedication of a Church," ch. 2, no. 84; cf. DCA, "Dedication of a Church Already in General Use for Sacred Celebrations," ch. 3, no. 39.

18. Cf. DCA, "Dedication of a Church," ch. 2, no. 1.

19. DCA, "Dedication of a Church," ch. 2, no. 1.

20. DCA, "Laying of a Foundation Stone or Commencement of Work on the Building of a Church," ch. 1, no. 22.

21. DCA:C, 6.

22. DCA, "Dedication of a Church," ch. 2, no. 2.

23. Ibid., no. 77.

24. Ibid., no. 75.

25. Ibid.

26. DCA, "Dedication of a Church Already in General Use for Sacred Celebrations," ch. 3, no. 35.

27. DCA, "Dedication of a Church," ch. 2, no. 75.

28. Ibid.

29. EACW, no. 39.

30. DCA, "Dedication of a Church," ch. 2, no. 15; cf. DCA, "Dedication of a Church," ch. 2, no. 17.

31. EACW, no. 41.
32. Cf. DCA, "Dedication of a Church," ch. 2, no. 11.
33. Ibid.
34. DCA:C, 7.
35. Ibid.
36. Ibid.
37. DCA, "Dedication of a Church," ch. 2, no. 30.
38. DCA:C, 8; cf. DCA, "Dedication of a Church," ch. 2, no. 30.
39. Ibid.
40. DCA, "Dedication of a Church," ch. 2, no. 31.
41. Ibid., no. 32.
42. DCA:C, 9.
43. Ibid.
44. Ibid.
45. Ibid.
46. DCA, "Dedication of a Church," ch. 2, no. 33.
47. DCA:C, 9.
48. Ibid., 10.
49. Cf. DCA:C, 10.
50. DCA:C, 10.
51. Ibid.
52. Ibid.
53. DCA, "Dedication of a Church," ch. 2, no. 33.
54. DCA:C, 10.
55. Ibid., 11.
56. DCA, "Dedication of a Church," ch. 2, no. 34.
57. DCA:C, 11.
58. DCA, "Dedication of a Church," ch. 2, no. 34.
59. DCA:C, 11–12.
60. DCA, "Dedication of a Church Already in General Use for Sacred Celebrations," ch. 3, no. 2.
61. CSL, no. 21.
62. DCA, "Dedication of a Church," ch. 2, no. 36.
63. Cf. DCA, "Dedication of a Church," ch. 2, nos. 37–42.
64. DCA, "Dedication of a Church," ch. 2, no. 11.
65. Ibid., no. 43.
66. Cf. DCA, "Dedication of a Church," ch. 2, nos. 44–47.
67. DCA, "Dedication of a Church," ch. 2, no. 4.
68. Ibid., no. 3; cf. CCL, 932:1.
69. EACW, no. 42.
70. EACW, no. 78.
71. GIRM, no. 257.
72. EACW, no. 53.
73. Ibid., no. 52.
74. GIRM, no. 257.

75. Cf. DCA, "Dedication of a Church," ch. 2, no. 3.
76. EACW, no. 62.
77. Ibid., no. 63.
78. Ibid., no. 62.
79. Ibid.
80. Ibid, no. 50.
81. Ibid.
82. Ibid.
83. Ibid., no. 58.
84. Ibid., no. 51.
85. Ibid.
86. MCW, no. 23.
87. EACW, no. 68.
88. Ibid., no. 58.
89. Ibid.
90. Ibid., no. 56.
91. Ibid.
92. Ibid., nos. 57–58.
93. Ibid., no. 59.
94. GIRM, no. 279.
95. EACW, no. 14.
96. Ibid., no. 54.
97. GIRM, no. 280.

Chapter 2

The Altar Is Christ

Ecclesial Documents

The norm of active participation is fleshed out in three documents that deal with the altar in the church: (1) the General Instruction of the Roman Missal, (2) *Environment and Art in Catholic Worship,* and (3) the rite for the *Dedication of a Church and an Altar.*

The General Instruction of the Roman Missal states, "The people of God assembled at Mass possess an organic and hierarchical structure, expressed by the various ministries and actions for each part of the celebration. The general plan of the sacred edifice should be such that in some way it conveys the image of the gathered assembly."[1] Even though the various members of the assembly "take the place most appropriate to them" in order "to carry out their individual functions properly," the ministries and actions of individuals "should at the same time form a complete and organic unity, clearly expressive of the unity of the entire holy people. The character and beauty of the place and all its appointments should foster devotion and show the holiness of the mysteries celebrated there."[2]

The rite for the *Dedication of a Church and an Altar* states: "The general plan of the sacred building should be such that it reflects in some way the whole assembly. It should allow for the distribution of all in due order and facilitate each one's proper function."[3]

Our consideration here is the theology of the altar found in the documents of the Church and the praxis which should flow from this theology. Praxis either fosters or impedes active participation.

35

It must be noted that the dedication of an altar usually takes place within the rite of a dedication of a church. However, since the focus is on the altar, only the texts that deal with the altar will be treated. It cannot be forgotten that "all of the local Church is gathered together" for the dedication of a church and an altar, "because all of it, hierarchically structured with its diversity of ministers and functions, is the celebrant of the rite of dedication."[4]

Theology of the Altar

A Holy Table

"At the altar the sacrifice of the cross is made present under sacramental signs,"[5] declares the General Instruction of the Roman Missal. "It is also the table of the Lord and the people of God are called together to share in it. The altar is, as well, the center of the thanksgiving that the eucharist accomplishes."[6]

Environment and Art in Catholic Worship emphasizes the table dimension of the altar. "The altar, the holy table, should be the most noble, the most beautifully designed and constructed table the community can provide. It is the common table of the assembly, a symbol of the Lord. . . . It is holy and sacred to this assembly's action and sharing."[7] "The altar is designed and constructed for the action of a community."[8]

The rite of the *Dedication of a Church and an Altar* also emphasizes the importance of the altar as a table. The prayer of dedication refers to the altar as "a ready table for the sacrifice of Christ."[9] On behalf of the community the bishop prays,

> Here may your children,
> gathered around your altar,
> celebrate the memorial of the Paschal Lamb,
> and be fed at the table of Christ's word and Christ's body.[10]

When only an altar is dedicated, in the prayer of dedication, after recalling the altars built by Noah, Abraham, and Moses, the bishop prays,

> Bless this altar built in the house of the Church,
> that it may ever be reserved for the sacrifice of Christ,
> and stand for ever as the Lord's table,
> where your people will find nourishment and strength.[11]

Throughout the rest of the prayer the altar is referred to as "a table of joy," "a place of communion and peace," "a source of unity and friendship," and "the center of . . . praise and thanksgiving."[12]

The preface of the Eucharistic Prayer used when dedicating an altar states,

> Here is prepared the Lord's table,
> at which your children,
> nourished by the body of Christ,
> are gathered into a Church, one and holy.[13]

When a place of worship is to be blessed because the building is only temporary, the prayer for the blessing of the altar declares,

> May it be the table
> at which we break the bread which gives us life
> and drink the cup which makes us one.[14]

Besides the references to the altar as a table found in the prayers for the "Dedication of an Altar," the introduction to the rite offers a wealth of explanation and insight. "When Christ the Lord instituted a memorial of the sacrifice he was about to offer the Father on the altar of the cross in the form of a sacrificial banquet, he made holy the table where the community would come to celebrate their Passover. Therefore the altar is the table of the sacrifice and the banquet."[15]

> "Everywhere . . . the Church's children can celebrate the memorial of Christ and take their place at the Lord's table. The Christian altar is by its very nature

a table of sacrifice and at the same time a table of the paschal banquet:
—a unique altar on which the sacrifice of the cross is perpetuated in mystery throughout the ages until Christ comes;
—a table at which the Church's children assemble to give thanks to God and receive the body and blood of Christ.[16]

"The entire dignity of an altar consists in this: the altar is the table of the Lord."[17]

Fixed and Movable Altars

According to the General Instruction of the Roman Missal, there are two types of altars—fixed and movable. "A fixed altar is one attached to the floor so that it cannot be moved; a movable altar is one that can be transferred from place to place."[18] "It is desirable that in every church there should be a fixed altar and that in other places set apart for sacred celebrations there should be either a fixed or a movable altar."[19]

No matter whether the altar is fixed or movable, it is to "be freestanding to allow the ministers to walk around it easily" and to permit the Eucharist "to be celebrated facing the people."[20] It "should be constructed away from the wall"[21] so that "it stands free, approachable from every side, capable of being encircled."[22]

Only One Altar

"In new churches it is better to erect one altar only, so that in the one assembly of the people of God the one altar may signify our one Savior Jesus Christ and the one eucharist of the Church."[23] If there is a chapel where the Eucharist is celebrated on weekdays with a small assembly of people, another altar may be erected there. However, a chapel should be "separated in some way from the body of the church."[24] "The erection of several altars in a church merely for the sake of adornment must be entirely avoided."[25] To place more than one altar in a church renders its symbolic function negligible. "The liturgical space has room for but one."[26]

The altar is not designed for concelebration. "The holy table . . . should not be elongated, but square or slightly rectangular, an attractive, impressive, dignified, noble table, constructed with solid and beautiful materials, in pure and simple proportions."[27]

The table of a fixed altar, "in accordance with the received custom of the Church and the biblical symbolism connected with an altar, . . . should be of stone, indeed natural stone."[28] However, "any becoming, solid, and skillfully constructed material"[29] may be used in erecting a fixed altar or a movable altar.[30] "The supports or pedestal for upholding the table may be made from any sort of material provided it is becoming and durable"[31] and "solid."[32]

PLACEMENT OF THE ALTAR

The altar is so placed in the church "as to be a focal point on which the attention of the whole congregation centers naturally."[33] However, this does not mean that "it must be spatially in the center or on a central axis. In fact, an off-center location may be a good solution in many cases. Placement and elevation must take into account the necessity of visibility and audibility for all."[34]

Relics

The General Instruction of the Roman Missal states that "it is fitting to maintain the practice of enclosing in the altar or of placing under the altar relics of saints, even of non martyrs."[35] The introduction to the rite for the "Dedication of an Altar" makes it clear that "it is not . . . the bodies of the martyrs that render the altar glorious; it is the altar that renders the burial place of the martyrs glorious."[36] Therefore, the relics intended for deposition "should be of such a size that they can be recognized as parts of human bodies. Hence excessively small relics of one or more saints must not be deposited." Furthermore: "The greatest care must be taken to determine whether relics intended for deposition are authentic. It is better for an altar to be dedicated without relics than to have relics of doubtful credibility placed beneath it." Finally, "a reliquary must not be placed on the altar or in the table of the altar but beneath the table of the altar."[37]

These regulations concerning relics abrogate previous norms which required that movable altars possess altar stones. "There is no obligation to have a consecrated stone in a movable altar or on the table where the eucharist is celebrated outside a place of worship."[38] The deposition of relics "beneath the table of the altar"[39] or the construction of an altar over the tomb of a martyr[40] is meant to emphasize that "the altar is dedicated to the one God by its very nature, for the eucharistic sacrifice is offered to the one God. It is in this sense that the Church's practice of dedicating altars to God in honor of the saints must be understood."[41]

The introduction to the rite for the "Dedication of an Altar" quotes St. Augustine in order to emphasize this point: "It is not to any of the martyrs, but to the God of the martyrs, though in memory of the martyrs, that we raise our altars."[42] Therefore, "in new churches statues and pictures of saints may not be placed over the altar. Likewise relics of saints should not be placed on the table of the altar when they are exposed for the veneration of the people."[43]

Dedication of an Altar

Not only is the dignity of the altar stressed in the documents that legislate its specifics concerning type, size, material, etc., but the rite of the "Dedication of an Altar" further upholds the fact that the table of the Lord is not only "a sign of Christ"[44] but "the altar is Christ."[45] The altar is treated as if it were a person to be initiated into the Church. While "the celebration of the eucharist is the most important rite, and the only necessary one, for the dedication of an altar,"[46] in accordance with the common tradition of the Church a special prayer of dedication is said and special rites are performed. Therefore, "care should be taken that Mass is not celebrated on a new altar before it has been dedicated."[47]

"BAPTISM" OF THE ALTAR

Instead of a penitential rite, the Mass of Dedication features a special rite of the blessing and sprinkling of water. In the introduction to this rite, the bishop instructs the faithful to "ask God to bless [the] gift of water. As it is sprinkled upon [the people] and upon [the] altar," the bishop instructs that it will "be a sign of . . . repentance and a reminder of . . . baptism."[48] In the prayer of blessing itself, the bishop addresses the "God of mercy," who has

> . . . established an inheritance of such mercy,
> that those sinners, who pass through water made sacred,
> die with Christ to rise restored
> as members of his body
> and heirs of his eternal covenant.[49]

Later in the same prayer, the bishop prays,

> As [the water] is sprinkled upon [all] and upon [the] altar
> make it a sign of the saving waters of baptism,
> by which [all] become one in Christ, the temple of [the] Spirit.[50]

After the prayer of blessing is finished, "the bishop passes through the main body of the church, sprinkling the people with the holy water; then, when he has returned to the sanctuary, he sprinkles the altar."[51] In this way, as can be seen, not only is the participation in the paschal mystery of death and resurrection through the water of baptism made reference to, but the altar is "baptized."

LITANY OF SAINTS

Following the Liturgy of the Word, the homily, and the profession of faith, the Litany of Saints is sung. Immediately following the litany, "the relics of martyrs or other saints are placed beneath the altar; this is to signify that all who have been baptized in the death of Christ, especially those who have shed their blood for the Lord, share in Christ's passion."[52] In this way, "the triumphant victims may occupy the place where Christ is victim: he, however, who suffered for all, upon the altar; they, who have been redeemed by his sufferings, beneath the altar."[53]

PRAYER OF DEDICATION

The prayer of dedication immediately follows. Besides the mention made above to this prayer in reference to the altar as the Lord's table, the prayer highlights the altar as

. . . a sign of Christ
from whose pierced side flowed blood and water,
which ushered in the sacraments of the Church.[54]

The reference to water immediately harkens back to the earlier "baptism" of the altar as well as to the post-death scene in the Gospel of John. The reference to blood points back to the Exodus account of the covenant-making ceremony, in which Moses took the blood of bulls and sprinkled it on the people and splashed it on the altar, and it points forward to the first Eucharist to be celebrated on the altar.

ANOINTING WITH CHRISM

The altar is anointed with the oil of chrism. "In virtue of the anointing with chrism the altar becomes a symbol of Christ who, before all others, is and is called 'The Anointed One'; for the Father anointed him with the Holy Spirit and constituted him the High Priest who on the altar of his body would offer the sacrifice of his life for the salvation of all."[55] Just as a newly baptized person is anointed on the head with the oil of chrism, and just as a person is confirmed by being reanointed on the forehead with the oil of chrism, so does the bishop pour chrism "on the middle of the altar and on each of its four corners, and it is recommended that he anoint the entire table of the altar."[56]

In order to develop the significance of the anointing with the oil of chrism, a trip back to the previous Holy Thursday celebration of the Chrism Mass is necessary. During this once-a-year liturgy, the Ordinary of a diocese consecrates the chrism. In the first of the two choices for consecratory prayers, the bishops prays:

> And so, Father, we ask you to bless ✛ this oil you have created.
> Fill it with the power of your Holy Spirit
> through Christ your Son.
> It is from him that chrism takes it name
> and with chrism you have anointed
> for yourself priests and kings,
> prophets and martyrs.
>
> Make this chrism a sign of life and salvation
> for those who are to be born again in the waters of baptism. . . .
> and when they are anointed with this holy oil
> make them temples of your glory,
> radiant with the goodness of life
> that has its source in you.
>
> Through this sign of chrism
> grant them royal, priestly, and prophetic honor,
> and clothe them with incorruption.
> Let this be indeed the chrism of salvation
> for those who will be born again of water and the Holy Spirit.[57]

This first prayer stresses the fact of the Spirit becoming present in the form of the oil. Just as bread and wine become the Body and Blood of Christ, so the chrism oil becomes the Holy Spirit. In the earlier days of the Church a candle burned before the tabernacle which contained the chrism, just as a candle burns before the tabernacle of the Lord's presence today. The remnant of the tabernacle for the chrism is found in some older churches in a box imbedded in the sanctuary wall or placed in the sacristy, labeled *Olea Sanctae*—"Holy Oils."

The prayer quickly moves on to explain the origin of the name for the chrism—Christ—and those classes of people that it has singled out in the past. Then it immediately points forward to those who will be baptized and anointed with the oil during the Easter Vigil. With the anointing they become temples, tabernacles, of the Spirit as well as royal, priestly, and prophetic people. Thus, when the altar is anointed with this oil, it, like the people who are anointed with it, are christened, "Christed," made into "other Christs."

The second optional consecratory prayer for the chrism picks up the theme of the paschal mystery of Christ:

> By his suffering, dying, and rising to life
> he saved the human race.
> He sent your Spirit to fill the Church
> with every gift needed to complete your saving work.
>
> From that time forward, through the sign of holy chrism,
> you dispense your life and love to men [and women].
> By anointing them with the Spirit,
> you strengthen all who have been reborn in baptism.[58]

This prayer places more emphasis on the transforming power of the anointing.

> Through that anointing
> you transform them [who have been reborn in baptism]
>   into the likeness of Christ your Son
> and give them a share
> in his royal, priestly, and prophetic work.
>
> Pour out the gifts of your Holy Spirit
> on our brothers and sisters who will be anointed with it.[59]

Thus the altar, anointed with the chrism, is transformed into the "likeness of Christ."

INCENSING THE ALTAR

After it has been "baptized" and "confirmed," "incense is burned on the altar to signify that the sacrifice of Christ, which is there perpetuated in mystery, ascends to God as an odor of sweetness, and also as a sign that the prayers of the people rise up pleasing and acceptable, reaching to the throne of God."[60] However, after the "brazier is placed on the altar for burning incense" and "the bishop puts incense into the brazier," he also "puts incense into the censer and incenses the altar." Then, "he returns to the chair, is incensed, and then sits" while another "minister incenses the people."[61]

A number of points need to be noted. First, the "fire recalls the Holy Spirit, that fire sent upon the Church by Christ, risen and seated at his

Father's right hand (see Acts 2:1-3). This is the very same fire that consumes the eucharistic sacrifice on the altar."[62]

Second, "the fragrance acceptable to the Father is that which comes from Christ's Easter sacrifice," as found in the Letter to the Ephesians: " '[Christ] gave himself for us as an offering to God, a gift of pleasing fragrance' (5:2)."[63]

Third, the Book of Revelation indicates that incense is "a symbol of prayer that rises to God" (5:8; 8:3-4).[64] Therefore, the assembly is incensed. "This ritual sequence suggests that the 'temple of God' where we are to offer 'spiritual worship' (Rom 12:1) is the individual baptized Christian and, at the same time, the entire assembly."[65]

These three points are best summarized in the prayer said by the bishop:

> Lord,
> may our prayer ascend as incense in your sight.
> As this building is filled with fragrance
> so may your Church fill the world
> with the fragrance of Christ.[66]

Fourth, in the future when incense is used, it will not only recall the dedication of the altar but the dedication of every individual baptized person who forms the assembly of believers. When the altar is incensed, so are all the ministers and all the people incensed.

CLOTHING THE ALTAR

After the incensing the brazier is removed and the table of the altar is wiped clean with cloths. The altar is covered with a white cloth, flowers may be placed near it, and candles may be placed on it or near it.

> The covering of the altar indicates that the Christian altar is the altar of the eucharistic sacrifice and the table of the Lord; standing around it priests and people, in one and the same action but with a difference of function, celebrate the memorial of the death and resurrection of Christ and partake in the Lord's Supper. For this reason the altar is prepared as the table of the sacrificial banquet and adorned as for a feast. Thus, the decoration of the altar clearly signifies that it is the Lord's table at which all God's people meet with joy to be refreshed with divine food, namely the body and blood of Christ sacrificed.[67]

The direct parallel between the *Rite of Christian Initiation of Adults* and the *Rite of Baptism for Children* must not be missed. After baptism and chrismation, one is clothed in a white garment. After the altar is "baptized" and "chrismated," it, too, is dressed in Easter white. The altar has become "a new creation"; it has been "clothed . . . in Christ."[68]

LIGHTING THE ALTAR

Immediately after the clothing in the white garment, the newly baptized receive a candle lighted from the Easter candle. The presider instructs them by saying,

> You have been enlightened by Christ.
> Walk always as children of the light
> and keep the flame of faith alive in your hearts.[69]

Likewise, after the altar is clothed in white, the candles on or near it along with those throughout the church are lighted. This would include those candles placed before the crosses, which have been either carved into the wall of the church or placed on the walls to mark the spots where the walls have been anointed. "A small bracket should be fitted beneath each cross into which is fixed a small candlestick with a candle to be lighted."[70]

"The lighting of the altar teaches us that Christ is 'a light to enlighten the nations,' whose brightness shines out in the Church and through it upon the whole human family."[71]

The statement made by the bishop as he gives a lighted candle to the deacon, who will light the candles for the celebration of the Eucharist, echoes the lighting of the Easter candle during the Easter Vigil:

> Light of Christ,
> shine on this altar
> and be reflected by those
> who share at this table.[72]

Christ is the "light of the world" (John 8:12), but "the church [building] resplendent in light is a symbol of the Church, illumined by Christ, and of the heavenly Jerusalem whose lamp is the Lamb."[73]

Also, "all the lamps around the altar are lit."[74] There is an obvious echo here of the Easter Vigil. During the Easter Vigil, once the Easter candle has been prepared, all share the light of Christ by holding individual candles. After the Easter proclamation these individual candles are extinguished, only to be rekindled for the renewal of baptismal promises after the elect have been initiated into the Church through the waters of baptism and anointing with the Spirit.

THE CELEBRATION OF THE EUCHARIST

The next rite of the entire dedication-initiation process is the celebration of the Eucharist. "When the altar has been prepared, the bishop celebrates the eucharist, which is the principal and the most ancient part of the whole rite."[75] In fact, "the celebration of the eucharist is in the closest harmony with the rite of the dedication of an altar."[76] Three reasons are given for this.

First, "when the eucharist sacrifice is celebrated, the end for which the altar was erected is attained and manifested by particularly clear signs."[77] For this reason, once the gifts of bread and wine are brought forward and then prepared, the bishop "kisses the altar; . . . however, neither the gifts nor the altar are incensed."[78]

The prayer over the gifts further emphasizes this point. The bishop prays,

> Lord,
> send your Spirit upon this altar
> to sanctify these gifts;
> may he prepare our hearts
> to receive them worthily.[79]

Second, "the eucharist, which sanctifies the hearts of those who receive it, in a sense consecrates the altar."[80] In order to emphasize this latter point, St. John Chrysostom is quoted: "This altar is an object of wonder: by nature it is stone, but it is made holy when it receives the body of Christ."[81] The "golden-mouthed" saint speaks of the altar as a person who is receiving the Eucharist for the first time in order to complete the initiation process (baptism, chrismation, Eucharist).

Third, "the bond whereby the dedication of an altar is closely linked with the celebration of the eucharist is likewise evident from the fact that the proper preface of the Mass is, as it were, an integral part of the rite of the dedication of an altar."[82] The preface of the Eucharistic Prayer declares that Christ,

> true priest and true victim
> . . . offered himself to [the Father]
> on the altar of the cross
> and commanded us to celebrate
> that same sacrifice,
> until he comes again. . . .
> Here the sacrifice of Christ is offered in mystery,
> perfect praise is given to [the Father],

and our redemption is made continually present.
Here is prepared the Lord's table,
at which . . . children,
nourished by the body of Christ,
are gathered into a Church, one and holy.
Here . . . people drink of the Spirit,
the stream of living water,
flowing from the rock of Christ.
They will become, in him,
a worthy offering and a living altar.[83]

The preface not only recalls the paschal mystery (the suffering, death, and resurrection of Christ), but it also echoes the sprinkling of the altar with water, the anointing with the Spirit, and the table dimension of the altar, from which the children of the Church are fed.

The Christian Is an Altar

Not only is the altar "a sign of Christ,"[84] and not only is Christ "the priest, the altar, and the lamb of sacrifice,"[85] but "his members and disciples are also spiritual altars on which the sacrifice of a holy life is offered to God."[86] To support this understanding, the introduction to the rite for the "Dedication of an Altar" quotes the teaching of the Fathers of the Church: "Saint Ignatius of Antioch asks the Romans quite plainly: 'Grant me only this favor: let my blood be spilled in sacrifice to God, while there is still an altar ready'; Saint Polycarp exhorts widows to lead a life of holiness, for 'they are God's altar.' Among others, Saint Gregory the Great echoes these words when he says: 'What is God's altar if not the soul of those who lead good lives? . . . Rightly then, the heart of the just is said to be the altar of God.' "[87]

"Or according to another idea frequently used by the writers of the Church: Christians who give themselves to prayer, who offer petitions to God and present sacrifices of supplication, are the living stones from which the Lord Jesus builds the Church's altar."[88]

From the altar, then, flows the spirituality of the assembly and of the individual members of the church. "The altar is the ideal center of the ecclesial edifice: all leads to and all leads from the altar. The altar is the 'place of concentration' of the purest liturgical spirituality and the most intense Christian piety."[89] The rite for the *Dedication of a Church and an Altar* "consistently puts the people before the building: they take possession of the building; they, before the walls and altar, are honored with incense; their celebration of the Eucharist 'consecrates' the place.''[90]

This spirituality, as we have seen, is repeatedly emphasized in the ritual actions of dedicating an altar. Whatever ritual is enacted around the altar has already been celebrated with people. First, the sprinkling of the altar with water stimulates the assembly's spirit of conversion and recalls "the rite of baptism and the first steps of the Christian's journey: 'You must reform and be baptized, each one of you' (Acts 2:38).''[91]

Second, the "anointing of the members takes its meaning from the anointing of Christ the Head.''[92] Immediately after baptism the Christian is anointed as priest, prophet, and king. In confirmation the Christian is anointed with the special gifts of the Spirit. The anointing of the altar reminds the assembly of their repeated anointings. This is why the "anointing begins with the altar, symbol of Christ, and proceeds to the side walls, symbols of Christians, stones of the Church.''[93] "The altar and church, marked with the same chrism, become an expressive sign of the mystery of Christ and his Church, that is of 'the Anointed One' par excellence and his anointed people.''[94]

Third, any time the altar is incensed, the Christian is reminded that he or she is a gift of pleasing fragrance to God and "a living sacrifice of praise.''[95] Each person is a temple of God wherein spiritual worship is offered.

Fourth, the clothing of the altar in a white cloth echoes the garment of the new creation of baptism. In baptism the Christian, who has been "clothed . . . in Christ," is instructed to bring his or her baptismal garment "unstained to the judgment seat of our Lord Jesus Christ" so that he or she "may have everlasting life.''[96]

Fifth, the festive lighting of the altar reminds the Christian of the light of Christ received in baptism. Every time the altar is used, the lights near it are kindled. The Christian is to "keep the flame of faith alive" in his or her heart.[97] In a special way during the Easter Vigil the entire assembly shares the light of Christ with each other and with the newly baptized. All are to carry this light throughout the journey of their lives so that "when the Lord comes," they may be able to "go out to meet him with all the saints in the heavenly kingdom.''[98]

The best summary of this spirituality is from a commentary on the rite for the *Dedication of a Church and an Altar* found in the *International Commission on English in the Liturgy Newsletter*:

The rite of dedication as a whole is a many-layered symbol which primarily intends the renewal of the worshipers as they inaugurate the use of their local church with prayer. In this way, the sprinkling at the beginning becomes an occasion for the community to recall its baptismal commitment. The acts of anointing, incensation, and lighting of the altar are another illustration of this. The altar as the ancient architectural symbol of Christ is anointed, incensed, and lighted first. The spiritual commission, offering, and illumination which these actions represent are then carried into the body of the church, among the community itself. As the material stones are consecrated to their use, the living stones are lifted to a vision of their eternal purpose.[99]

Praxis

From this understanding of the theology of the altar, there flows a definite practice. As with all the revisions inaugurated by Vatican Council II, the theological background is given as a reason for the praxis which follows.

Only One Altar

Liturgical praxis would dictate that there be only one altar in a church. This is stated most clearly in the introduction to the rite for the "Dedication of an Altar": "In new churches it is better to erect one altar only, so that in the one assembly of the people of God the one altar may signify our one Savior Jesus Christ and the one eucharist of the Church."[100] This statement is not meant to be "a polemic against other epochs, when a different manner of worship and piety occasionally led to an exasperating proliferation of altars."[101] There is, however, an emphasis being placed on "a return to an older, more genuine custom, the only completely valid one from a liturgical point of view"—only one altar should be erected in new churches."[102]

This one altar should be fixed. Its table should be made of stone in order to signify the biblical references to Christ as the cornerstone and the foundation of the Church. Furthermore, it should be square or only slightly rectangular. No reason exists to continue past practices of carving into or attaching signs, symbols, or slogans to the altar. The way it is constructed as well as the materials used in its construction declare its dignity and purpose.

It must be noted here that in older churches where renovation has not removed the altar against the wall and has installed a freestanding altar enabling the presider to face the people, there is no "main altar" (usually a reference to the old one against the wall) and "another altar" (the one where the Eucharist is celebrated). Care must be taken that the altar against the wall is not decorated or highlighted even if the tabernacle has been left there. The altar against the wall is not the assembly's table. It should be completely free of candles, cloths, flowers, etc. To continue to enhance the altar against the wall with such items is to deliver a message to the community that cannot be supported by the theology of the altar as illustrated above. Only the one altar signifies the one assembly gathered around the one Savior.

Renewal of Baptism

Every Sunday the assembly is offered the opportunity to recall its baptismal commitment through celebration of the rite of blessing and sprinkling holy water. This rite "may be celebrated in all churches and chapels at all Sunday Masses celebrated on Sunday or on Saturday evening."[103] "When this rite is celebrated it takes the place of the penitential rite at the beginning of Mass."[104]

This weekly recalling of baptism should be frequently used throughout the year. Its relationship to the day of the dedication of the church is obvious, but more importantly, its relationship to the Easter Vigil is highlighted. After the elect are baptized and chrismated during the Easter Vigil, the entire assembly renews its baptismal promises and is sprinkled with water. In the United States "in Easter Sunday Masses . . . the rite of the renewal of baptismal promises is repeated after the homily" and the people are sprinkled "with the blessed water."[105]

Incense

Because "the use of incense is optional in any form of Mass,"[106] it should be used especially on Sundays, solemnities, and feasts in order to recall the dedication of the altar and to remind the assembly of its dedication. After arriving at the altar, the presider "incenses the altar while circling it."[107] This recalls the day of the dedication of the altar.

After the gifts of bread and wine have been collected and prepared on the altar, "the gifts on the altar and the altar itself may be incensed. This is a symbol of the Church's offering and prayer going up to God. Afterward the deacon or other minister may incense the priest and the people."[108] The people are reminded that they are spiritual altars dedicated to God and living sacrifices of praise.

Altar Clothing

The clothing of the altar should be especially considered. Its white cloth is a reminder to the assembly of the unstained garments received in baptism—garments to be kept pure and white until the day of Jesus Christ. For this reason "at least one cloth should be placed on the altar out of reverence for the celebration of the memorial of the Lord and the banquet that gives us his body and blood. The shape, size, and decoration of the altar cloth should be in keeping with the design of the altar."[109]

A simple white cloth without lots of lace or frill would be in keeping with the spirit of this directive. The vesture of the altar should not be like that of " 'frontals' or 'facades,' but as decorative covering which respects the integrity and totality" of the altar.[110] Signs, symbols, or slogans should not be embroidered or painted onto the cloth. Such items echo the days of elaborately decorated antependia—silk altar frontals filled with signs and symbols—and altar covers displaying slogans outlined in script embroidery. These items definitely detract from the integrity of the altar.

While a white cloth in remembrance of baptism is recommended for the usual altar covering, cloths or vesture of other colors to be used during specific liturgical seasons are not excluded. The use of a light violet during Advent and a dark purple during Lent as well as a bright green during Ordinary Time can enhance the dignity of the altar. During the Easter season, however, white would seem to be the only appropriate color due to its connection with the baptismal themes that occur through this season.

Candles

"Candles are to be used at every liturgical service as a sign of reverence and festiveness. The candles are to be placed either on or around the altar in a way suited to the design of the altar and the sanctuary. Everything is to be well balanced and must not interfere with the faithful's clear view of what goes on at the altar or is placed on it."[111]

Since only two candles are needed for the celebration of any Eucharist, an alternative to placing the candles on the altar is to locate them near the altar. This does not mean that they have to be on either side of the altar—for placing them together on one side in an artistic arrangement can be aesthetically pleasing—nor does it mean that they have to be within twelve inches of the altar—for often the arrangement of a church building offers opportunities to place the candles in a variety of locations. "When they are free-standing, they can be arranged differently from time to time." Also, "the number can be varied according to the season and feast and the solemnity of the celebration." Likewise, "the candles should be visible without impeding the sight of the altar, ambo, chair and action."[112]

All candles used in the celebration of the Eucharist and in any other liturgical rites are to be "made of wax."[113] "Because of their very nature, imitations of candles should not be used in the liturgy as, for example, 'permanent' paschal candles, etc. Nor should electrical bulbs be used in liturgical celebration. . . . The use of . . . other material either in substitutes for or in imitations of candles is not permitted in the liturgy."[114] Oil lamps may not be used. Nothing can satisfy the demand for integrity in lights for liturgical use other than candles made of wax.

One Cross

The General Instruction of the Roman Missal states that "there is . . . to be a cross, clearly visible to the congregation, either on the altar or near it."[115] Appendix 1 to the General Instruction for the Dioceses of the United States of America emphasizes that this cross should be the one "carried in a procession in order to give greater dignity and reverence to the cross."[116] Thus the cross carried in procession is placed near the altar "so that it may serve as the cross of the altar. Otherwise it should be put away during the service."[117]

Environment and Art in Catholic Worship further explains the reason for using only one cross. "A cross is a basic symbol in any Christian liturgical celebration. The advantage of a processional cross with a floor standard, in contrast to one that is permanently hung or affixed to a wall, is that it can be placed differently according to the celebration and the other environmental factors. While it is permissible for the cross to rest on the altar, it is preferable that it be elsewhere, not only for non-eucharistic liturgies but also so that in eucharistic celebrations the altar is used only for bread and wine and book."[118]

By carrying in procession the cross that is to be placed near the altar, not only is the cross given respect but the altar is respected as a holy table upon which are placed only "the bread and wine and their vessels and the book."[119] By placing the free-standing cross somewhere near the altar, the altar can "stand free, approachable from every side, capable of being encircled."[120]

Furthermore, "the multiplication of crosses in a liturgical space or as ornamentation on objects may lessen rather than increase attention to that symbol. The multiplication of symbols causes their very diminution."[121]

Not a Table of Convenience

The altar "is never used as a table of convenience or as a resting place for papers, notes, cruets, or anything else."[122] Only the corporal, purificator, missal, chalice, and bread are placed on the altar.[123] "Other gifts for the church or the poor brought by the faithful or collected at the Mass . . . are to be put in a suitable place but not on the altar."[124] Furthermore, in order to continuously emphasize the dignity of the altar, "in new churches statues and pictures of saints may not be placed over the altar. Likewise, relics of saints should not be placed on the table of the altar when they are exposed for the veneration of the people."[125]

Finally, "suitable decoration need not and should not be confined to the altar area, since the unity of the celebration space and the active participation of the entire assembly are fundamental principles. Both beauty and

simplicity demand careful attention to each piece of furniture, each object, each decorative element, as well as to the whole ensemble, so that there is no clutter, no crowding. These various objects and elements must be able to breathe and function without being smothered by excess.''[126]

For this reason ''it is desirable that candles, cross, any flowers or other decoration in the area should not be so close to the altar as to constitute impediments to anyone's approach or movement around the common table.''[127] ''Flowers, plants and trees—genuine, of course—are particularly apt for the decoration of liturgical space, since they are of nature, always discreet in their message, never cheap or tawdry or ill-made. Decoration should never impede the approach to or the encircling of the altar or any of the ritual movement and action, but there are places in most liturgical spaces where it is appropriate and where it can be enhancing. The whole space is to be considered the arena of decoration, not merely the sanctuary.''[128]

Since ''audibility and visibility to all in the assembly are minimal requirements,''[129] anything that hinders these should not be near the altar.[130]

This directive certainly eliminates bouquets of flowers placed in front of the altar, nativity scenes erected in front of the altar, banners pinned to the altar, huge microphones set upon the altar, or large bookstands resting on the altar. Large items either in front of or on the altar create psychological blockades; these push the assembly away from its common table while also pushing the table away from the assembly. An altar with something in front of it tells people to stay away; it might as well be roped off. Certainly this cannot be said to foster participation, nor does such practice flow from the theology of the altar as outlined above.

Conclusion

In general, the reverence shown to the altar flows from the theology of the altar as found in the documents of the Church. The theology of the altar should inform praxis, which includes anything that is even remotely near the altar. In his or her relationship to the altar, every Christian must remember that the altar is Christ and that he or she is a spiritual altar whose purpose exists in participating in worship around the assembly's common table.

Notes

1. GIRM, no. 257.
2. Ibid.
3. DCA, "Dedication of a Church," ch. 2, no. 3.
4. DCA:C, 7.
5. GIRM, no. 259.
6. Ibid.
7. EACW, no. 71.
8. Ibid., no. 72.
9. DCA, "Dedication of a Church," ch. 2, no. 62.
10. Ibid.
11. DCA, "Dedication of an Altar," ch. 4, no. 48.
12. Ibid.
13. Ibid., no. 60.
14. DCA, "Blessing of a Church," ch. 5, no. 21.
15. DCA, "Dedication of an Altar," ch. 4, no. 3.
16. Ibid., no. 4.
17. Ibid., no. 5.
18. GIRM, no. 261; cf. CCL, 1235:1.
19. DCA, "Dedication of an Altar," ch. 4, no. 6; cf. CCL, 1235:2.
20. GIRM, no. 262.
21. DCA, "Dedication of an Altar," ch. 4, no. 8.
22. EACW, no. 71.
23. DCA, "Dedication of an Altar," ch. 4, no. 7.
24. GIRM, no. 267.
25. DCA, "Dedication of an Altar," ch. 4, no. 7.
26. EACW, no. 72.
27. Ibid.
28. DCA, "Dedication of an Altar," ch. 4, no. 9; cf. GIRM, no. 263; cf. CCL, 1236:1.
29. Ibid.
30. Cf. GIRM, no. 264; cf. CCL, 1236:2.
31. DCA, "Dedication of an Altar,"ch. 4, no. 9.
32. GIRM, no. 263.
33. GIRM, no. 262.
34. EACW, no. 73.
35. GIRM, no. 266; cf. CCL, 1237:2.
36. DCA, "Dedication of an Altar," ch. 4, no. 5.
37. Ibid., no. 11; cf. CCL, 1239:2.
38. GIRM, no. 265.
39. DCA, "Dedication of an Altar," ch. 4, no. 11.
40. Cf. DCA, "Dedication of an Altar," ch. 4, no. 5.
41. DCA, "Dedication of an Altar," ch. 4, no. 10.
42. Ibid.

43. Ibid.
44. Ibid., no. 48.
45. Ibid., no. 4.
46. Ibid., no. 21.
47. Ibid., no. 13; cf. CCL, 932:2 and 1237:1.
48. Ibid., no. 35.
49. Ibid.
50. Ibid.
51. Ibid., no. 36.
52. Ibid., no. 20.
53. Ibid., no. 5.
54. Ibid., no. 48.
55. Ibid., no. 22.
56. Ibid., no. 49.
57. TS: RBOCC, no. 25.
58. Ibid.
59. Ibid.
60. DCA, "Dedication of an Altar," ch. 4, no. 22.
61. Ibid., no. 53.
62. DCA:C, 29.
63. Ibid.
64. Ibid.
65. Ibid., 29–30.
66. DCA, "Dedication of an Altar," ch.4, no. 53.
67. Ibid., no. 22; cf. CCL, 1239:1.
68. RCIA, no. 229.
69. Ibid., no. 230.
70. DCA, "Dedication of a Church," ch. 2, no. 22.
71. DCA, "Dedication of an Altar," ch. 4, no. 22.
72. Ibid., no. 55.
73. DCA:C, 31.
74. DCA, "Dedication of an Altar," ch. 4, no. 23.
75. Ibid., no. 23.
76. Ibid.
77. Ibid.
78. Ibid., no. 58.
79. Ibid., no. 59.
80. Ibid., no. 23.
81. Ibid.
82. Ibid.
83. Ibid., no. 60.
84. Ibid., no. 48.
85. TS, Preface of Easter V.
86. DCA, "Dedication of an Altar," ch. 4, no. 2.
87. Ibid.

88. Ibid.

89. DCA:C, 25.

90. John Allyn Melloh, "The Rite of Dedication," *Assembly* 10, no. 2 (November 1983) 232.

91. DCA:C, 13.

92. Ibid., 27.

93. Ibid.

94. Ibid.

95. TS, Eucharistic Prayer IV.

96. RCIA, no. 229.

97. Ibid., no. 230.

98. Ibid.

99. "Rite for the Dedication of a Church: A Commentary," *Newsletter: International Commission on English in the Liturgy* 4, no. 4 (October–December 1977) 3.

100. DCA, "Dedication of an Altar," ch. 4, no. 7.

101. DCA:C, 26.

102. Ibid.

103. TS, Appendix I, Rite of Blessing and Sprinkling Holy Water, no. 1.

104. Ibid.

105. TS, Easter Sunday, Renewal of Baptismal Promises.

106. GIRM, no. 235.

107. Ibid., no. 85.

108. Ibid., no. 51.

109. Ibid., no. 268.

110. EACW, no. 95.

111. GIRM, no. 269.

112. EACW, no. 89.

113. BCLN 20 (November 1984) 44.

114. Ibid.

115. GIRM, no. 270.

116. GIRM, Appendix 1, no. 270.

117. Ibid.

118. EACW, no. 88.

119. Ibid., no. 71.

120. Ibid.

121. Ibid., no. 86.

122. Ibid., no. 71.

123. Cf. GIRM, no. 49.

124. GIRM, no. 49.

125. DCA, "Dedication of an Altar," ch. 4, no. 10.

126. EACW, no. 103.

127. Ibid., no. 71.

128. Ibid., no. 102.

129. Ibid., no. 61.

130. Cf. EACW, nos. 61 and 63; GIRM, no. 269.

Chapter 3

The Table of the Word of God

Ecclesial Documents

The norm of active participation in reference to the ambo is stated in five documents: (1) the General Instruction of the Roman Missal, (2) *Environment and Art in Catholic Worship*, (3) the rite for the *Dedication of a Church and an Altar*, (4) the Introduction to the Lectionary for Mass, and (5) the "Order for the Blessing of a New Lectern" as found in the *Book of Blessings*.

The Introduction to the Lectionary for Mass states that "the faithful at the celebration of Mass are to listen to the word of God with an inward and outward reverence."[1] "Accordingly, the faithful's participation in the liturgy increases to the degree that as they listen to the word of God spoken in the liturgy they strive harder to commit themselves to the Word of God made flesh in Christ."[2]

The people also participate by singing the responsorial psalm: "To foster the congregation's singing, every means available in the various cultures is to be employed."[3] The document declares that "in the hearing of God's word the Church is built up and grows."[4]

For a new lectern, the "Order of Blessing Within a Celebration of the Word of God," found in the *Book of Blessings*, offers a brief address given to the people by the presider in order to prepare them for the celebration and to explain the meaning of the rite: "Let us take part in this celebration attentively, listening faithfully to God speaking to us, so that his words may truly become for us spirit and life."[5]

Our consideration here is the theology of the ambo (also referred to as the lectern or the pulpit) found in the documents of the Church and the praxis which should flow from this theology. After exploring the theology of the word presented by Vatican Council II, the praxis, which either fosters or impedes active participation, will be examined.

It must be noted that the blessing of an ambo, the table of the word, usually takes places within the rite of a dedication of a church. "When a church is dedicated or blessed, all the appointments that are already in place are considered to be blessed along with the church."[6] However, when "the lectern for proclamation of the word . . . [is] newly installed or renovated, there is an opportunity to teach the faithful the importance of such [an] appointment by means of the celebration of a blessing."[7] Since our focus is on the ambo, we will only treat the texts that deal with the ambo.

Theology of the Word

Restoration of Scripture

The Constitution on the Sacred Liturgy of Vatican Council II declares that "in sacred celebrations a more ample, more varied, and more suitable reading from sacred scripture should be restored."[8] The three-year Lectionary cycle for Sundays, the two-year cycle for weekdays, the "Commons," "Ritual Masses," "Masses for Various Occasions," and "Votive Masses" selections found in the Lectionary, along with the multiple choices for Scripture readings found in *Pastoral Care of the Sick: Rite of Anointing and Viaticum,* the revised *Rite of Christian Initiation of Adults,* the revised *Order of Christian Funerals,* and the *Book of Blessings,* not only attest to the importance of the Liturgy of the Word in any celebration but fulfill the mandate of The Constitution on the Sacred Liturgy: "The treasures of the Bible are to be opened up more lavishly so that a richer fare may be provided for the faithful at the table of God's word."[9]

Sign and Symbol of the Word

Every ritual can be subdivided into sign and symbol. A sign is a thing, object, person, or circumstance that represents or points toward another thing, object, person, or circumstance. In contrast, a symbol is an action that reveals a relationship; it is not a thing. For example, either the Lectionary, the Book of Gospels, or a Bible is a sign of God's word, but the symbol is the proclamation and hearing of that Word wherein God reveals his/her constantly offered friendship and covenants to people.[10] "Hearing the word of God unceasingly proclaimed arouses . . . faith."[11]

"The Scriptures, and above all in their liturgical proclamation, are the source of life and power. . . . When this word is proclaimed in the Church and put into living practice, it enlightens the faithful through the working of the Holy Spirit and draws them into the entire mystery of the Lord as a reality to be lived. The word of God reverently received moves the heart and its desires toward conversion and toward a life filled with both individual and community faith, since God's word is the sustenance of the Christian life and the source of the prayer of the entire Church."[12]

Some of the people participate in the liturgical proclamation of the word by reading the assigned pericopes. The entire assembly is engaged "by means of acclamations, responses, psalms, antiphons, hymns, as well as by actions, gestures and bodily attitudes."[13]Through these methods the liturgy becomes "an action of the entire people of God, hierarchically organized, and acting hierarchically."[14]

This theology of the word (in the action of proclaiming and hearing the word) explains that God speaks to his people, who "receive the power to respond . . . actively with full faith, hope, and charity through prayer and self-giving . . . in their entire Christian life."[15]

Theology of the Ambo

Environment and Art in Catholic Worship reminds us that "every word, gesture, movement, object, appointment must be real in the sense that it is our own. It must come from the deepest understanding of ourselves."[16] This "deepest understanding of ourselves" is reflected in the ambo, from where the Word of God is proclaimed. "The liturgical celebration, based primarily on the word of God and sustained by it, becomes a new event and enriches the word itself with new meaning and power."[17] The ambo is "the symbol to us all of the table of God's word that provides the first and necessary nourishment for our Christian life."[18]

A Place for the Proclamation of the Word of God

The General Instruction of the Roman Missal states, "The dignity of the word of God requires the church to have a place that is suitable for proclamation of the word and is a natural focal point for the people during the liturgy of the word."[19] This place is to be "somewhat elevated, fixed, and of a suitable design and nobility. It should reflect the dignity of God's word and be a clear reminder to the people that in the Mass the table of God's word and of Christ's body is placed before them."[20]

This place is where the ambo is located. "The ambo or lectern is a stand-ings lay the table of God's word for the faithful and open up the riches of the Bible to them."[23] From the ambo the people have the opportunity ings lay the table of God's word for the faithful and open up the riches of the Bible to them."[23] From the ambo the people have the opportunity of "tasting the sweetness of [the] word" and being "filled with the love of [the] Son that surpasses all knowledge."[24] Therefore, "the ambo represents the dignity and uniqueness of the Word of God and of reflection upon that Word."[25]

Only One Ambo

Only "one main ambo should be reserved for these functions."[26] The one ambo is similar to the one altar. "In the one assembly of the people of God the one altar signifies our one Savior Jesus Christ and the one eucharist of the Church."[27] Similarly, the one ambo in the one assembly of the people of God signifies the one word of God in which "Christ is present . . . ; as he carries out the mystery of salvation, he sanctifies us and offers the Father perfect worship."[28]

"Moreover, the word of God unceasingly calls to mind and extends the plan of salvation, which achieves its fullest expression in the liturgy. The liturgical celebration becomes, therefore, the continuing, complete, and effective presentation of God's word.

"That word, constantly proclaimed in the liturgy is always, then, a living, active word through the power of the Holy Spirit. It expresses the Father's love that never fails in its effectiveness toward us."[29]

Furthermore, "when in celebrating the liturgy the Church proclaims both the Old and New Testament, it is proclaiming one and the same mystery of Christ."[30] "In hearing God's word the Church is built up and grows, and in the signs of the liturgical celebration God's many wonderful, past works in the history of salvation are symbolically presented anew. God in turn makes use of the assembly of the faithful who celebrate the liturgy in order that his word may speed on in triumph and his name be exalted among all peoples."[31]

Dedication of the Ambo

Because "the ambo represents the dignity and uniqueness of the Word of God and of reflection upon that Word,"[32] the rite of the dedication of the ambo, which takes place within the rite of the *Dedication of a Church and an Altar,* indicates that "the liturgy of the word has a value that is independent of its relationship to the celebration of the eucharist. . . . The community is born of the word, is nourished by it, and grows and develops by means of it."[33]

After the opening prayer of the rite of the *Dedication of a Church and an Altar,* "two readers, one of whom carries *The Lectionary,* and the psalmist come to the bishop. The bishop . . . takes *The Lectionary,* shows it to the people, and says:

May the word of God always be heard in this place,

as it unfolds the mystery of Christ before you
and achieves your salvation within the Church.

Then the bishop hands *The Lectionary* to the first reader. The readers and the psalmist proceed to the lectern, carrying *The Lectionary* for all to see."[34]

Three important points need to be made about this rite. First, "the honor shown to the book is shown to Christ, incarnate wisdom, the master who speaks whenever the Good News is proclaimed; in this way the display of the book proclaims the primacy of Christ, of his person and Gospel."[35]

Second, it is the use of the ambo which dedicates it. Only during this first time is the Lectionary carried to the ambo. In the future, the Lectionary will be prepared there before the celebration of the Eucharist begins.[36] Only the Book of Gospels, "if distinct from the book of the other readings," may be "carried in the entrance procession."[37]

Just as the celebration of the Eucharist "is the principal and the most ancient part of the whole rite"[38] of the "Dedication of an Altar," "for when the eucharistic sacrifice is celebrated, the end for which the altar was erected is attained and manifested by particularly clear signs"[39] (bread and wine), so is the first proclamation of the word of God from the ambo the principal part of the rite for dedicating the ambo. When the Lectionary is placed upon the ambo (like bread and wine are placed upon the altar), the end for which the ambo was erected is attained and manifested by the particularly clear signs of the Lectionary, the Book of Gospels, and the Bible.

Third, "the book is held up for all to see by the bishop, indicating that one of his first and chief duties is to proclaim the Gospel of Christ, and that 'the task . . . of authentically interpreting the word of God . . . has been entrusted exclusively to the living teaching office of the Church, whose authority is exercised in the name of Jesus Christ. This teaching office is not above the word of God but serves it' (Constitution on Divine Revelation, no. 10)."[40]

Blessing of the Ambo

This theology of the ambo is further fleshed out in the *Book of Blessings* in the "Order for the Blessing of a New Lectern." If the blessing takes place within Mass, "the Book of the Gospels is carried in the entrance procession and placed on the altar. Everything proceeds in the usual way up to and including the opening prayer."[41] After the opening prayer the same rite as outlined above for the dedication of the ambo is carried out. The only element that is different is that the assisting deacon, if there is one, or else the priest, "takes the Book of the Gospels from the altar and, preceded by candlebearers and censer bearer, carries it to the lectern."[42]

When a church and an altar are dedicated, "no lights are used apart from those which surround the relics of the saints, nor is incense used either in the procession or in the Mass before the rite of the incensation and the lighting of the altar and the church."[43] "The symbol of light is deliberately saved for this particular point, the moment of praise to Christ the light."[44] Since the blessing of a new lectern is envisioned as taking place in an already dedicated church, both light and incense are used.

When the blessing of a new lectern takes place outside of Mass, the rite for the "Order of Blessing Within a Celebration of the Word of God" is used. After the greeting the presider states that the blessing of the lectern will "begin its sacred use, namely, as the symbol . . . of the table of God's word that provides the first and necessary nourishment for . . . Christian life."[45] He encourages the people to take an attentive and active part in the blessing so that "listening faithfully to God speaking . . . , his words may truly become . . . spirit and life."[46]

The opening prayer, which asks God for "the grace of the Holy Spirit, so that" all may taste "the sweetness of [the] word,"[47] immediately follows. "Texts of sacred Scripture are then read, between which . . . there is a responsorial psalm or a period of silent reflection."[48] "In the homily the celebrant gives those present an explanation of the biblical text and of the truth that Christ is present in the word of God."[49]

The recitation of the profession of faith is optional.

Specific intercessions follow. The first asks that the Lord "give to the followers of Christ . . . a constant hunger for [the] word." The second is for all present that "by searching deeply into [the] word [they] may remain firmly convinced in faith and resolute in the desire to do what is right and good." The third petitions for "the light of [the] word" for knowledge of God and of self so that all will return God's love and serve God as they ought. The final intercession is for "the ministers of [the] word, so that what they preach they will believe in their hearts and manifest in their actions."[50]

The intercessions are concluded with a prayer of blessing, which is addressed to God. The prayer begins with a thanksgiving to God for having called people "out of darkness into . . . wonderful light." All are reminded that it is God who satisfies "the hunger" in hearts "with the sweet nourishment of [the] word." The petition is that those in the church "may listen to the voice of [the] Son, so that, responding to the inspiration of the Holy Spirit," they "may not be hearers only but doers of [the] word." The final petition is "that those who proclaim [the] message from [the] lectern may show [others] how to direct [their] lives, so that [they] will walk in the ways of Christ, following him faithfully until [they] reach eternal life."[51]

The order of blessing concludes with a prayer over the people in which the celebrant asks that the people be instructed "with the word of truth" and that their hearts be formed "with the Gospel of salvation."[52] The presider asks God to bless the people, and a suitable song concludes the celebration.[53]

It is to be noted that like the rite for the dedication of the ambo during the *Dedication of a Church and an Altar,* or like the rite for the blessing of an ambo within Mass, the rite for the blessing of an ambo within a celebration of the word of God highlights the fact that it is the actual proclamation of the word from the ambo that dedicates the ambo. There are no rubrics which indicate that the ambo is either signed with the cross, sprinkled with holy water, or incensed. It is the proclamation of the word of God that dedicates the ambo. "Whenever . . . the Church, gathered by the Holy Spirit for liturgical celebration, announces and proclaims the word of God, it has the experience of being a new people in whom the covenant made in the past is fulfilled."[54]

Praxis

From this understanding of the theology of the word and the ambo, there flows a definite practice. As with all the revisions inaugurated by Vatican Council II, the theological background is given as a reason for the praxis which follows.

A Place Reserved for the Proclamation of the Scriptures

Because it "reflects the dignity of God's word"[55] the ambo is "of its nature . . . reserved for the readings, the responsorial psalm, and the Easter Proclamation."[56] While it may also be used for the homily[57] and the general intercessions,[58] the homily can be delivered by the homilist at the chair either standing or sitting,[59] and the general intercessions can also be directed by the presider from his chair.[60] Since "it is desirable that a deacon, cantor, or other person announce the intentions"[61] if a deacon is present and leads the general intercessions, these can be announced from his chair. Otherwise, "the celebrant presides at the chair and the intentions are announced at the lectern."[62]

A Fixed Ambo

When building an ambo, the directive given in the General Instruction of the Roman Missal should be kept in mind: "As a rule the lectern or ambo should be stationary, not simply a movable stand."[63] In this way, the ambo is like the altar: "In every church there should be a fixed altar."[64] The "Order for the Blessing of a New Lectern" further emphasizes this point: "The present blessing may only be imparted to a true lectern, that is, not a simple, movable stand, but a lectern that is fixed."[65]

When erecting a fixed ambo, the same instruction given for a fixed altar applies. The location of the ambo "will be central in any eucharistic celebration, but this does not mean it must be spatially in the center or on a central axis."[66] Neither does this mean that it must always be located to the left of the altar. "Focus and importance in any celebration move with the movement of the rite. Placement and elevation must take into account the necessity of visibility and audibility for all."[67]

When a fixed ambo cannot be erected, "because of the architecture of a particular church, a lectern may have to be movable; . . . such a lectern may be blessed."[68] This point finds an echo in the same situation when an altar cannot be fixed: "In other places set apart for sacred celebrations there should be either a fixed or a movable altar."[69]

Design of the Ambo

The ambo, like the altar, "should be beautifully designed, constructed of fine materials, and proportioned carefully and simply for its function."[70] "In order that the lectern may properly serve its liturgical purpose, it is to be rather large, since on occasion several ministers must use it at the same time."[71] However, "great pains must . . . be taken, in keeping with the design of each church, over the harmonious and close relationship of the lectern with the altar,"[72] since it is from the table of the word and the table of the altar that the faithful are fed.[73] Furthermore, all of the furnishings of a church, taken together, "should possess a unity and harmony with each other and with the architecture of the place."[74]

The ambo, because it is to "truly help the people's listening and attention during the liturgy of the word,"[75] "must be so placed that the ministers may be easily seen and heard by the faithful."[76] "Provision must also be made for the readers to have enough light to read the text and, as required, to have sound equipment enabling the congregation to hear them without difficulty."[77]

Where All Scripture Texts Are Read

All of "the readings are always to be proclaimed at the lectern."[78] Never should the first two pericopes be proclaimed at one ambo and the gospel at another; only one main ambo is to be present in a church, just as there is but one altar in a church. What is at stake is the unity of the one word of God. The issue is not the number of liturgical books (Lectionary, Book of Gospels) that may be placed on or within the ambo but the reverence shown in decorating, handling, and reading from these books. All the Scriptures, both the Hebrew Bible and the New Testament, those proclaimed by a reader and those proclaimed by a deacon or priest, are read from the same ambo.

Since "the people of God have a spiritual right to receive abundantly from the treasury of God's word,"[79] "proper measures must . . . be taken to ensure that there are qualified laypersons who have been trained" to proclaim the readings.[80] Otherwise, how can the faithful "listen to the word of God with an inward and outward reverence that will bring them continuous growth in the spiritual life and draw them more deeply into the mystery they celebrate"?[81]

The unity of the Liturgy of the Word is found at the altar of the word, the ambo. The action of proclaiming the entire word from one ambo parallels the sharing that takes place from the one bread and the one cup on the one altar-table.

Decoration

"Either permanently or at least on occasions of greater solemnity, the lectern should be decorated simply and in keeping with its design."[82] Whatever is used as a type of vesture for the ambo, however, should not be as a frontal or a facade, "but as a decorative covering which respects [its] integrity and totality."[83] If a fabric is used, "it should be chosen because of the quality of design, texture and color."[84]

It is not appropriate to either permanently affix signs and symbols to the ambo or to the vesture on it. Furthermore, the ambo is not a place to hang a banner. The purpose of vesture for the ambo is to "appeal to the senses and thereby create an atmosphere and a mood."[85]

Out of place at the ambo would be a microphone that, due to its type or style, tends to dominate the space. Likewise the placement of flowers, nativity scenes, trees, plants, or anything else in front of the ambo creates a psychological blockade. Objects placed before the ambo psychologically and simultaneously push the ambo away from the assembly and the assembly away from the ambo. Certainly this arrangement cannot foster participation or respect for the inherent dignity of the ambo, the altar of the word of God.

Like the altar, the ambo "stands free, approachable from every side, capable of being encircled."[86] Decoration should never impede the approach to or the encircling of the ambo or any of the ritual movement and action, but there are places in most liturgical spaces where such decoration is appropriate and where it can be enhancing. The whole space of the church and not merely the sanctuary is to be considered the arena of decoration.[87]

On more solemn occasions, freestanding candles may be placed near the ambo; however, "near" does not mean within six inches. It must always be kept in mind that "candles, cross, any flowers or other decoration in the area should not be so close . . . as to constitute impediments to anyone's approach or movement around the common table"[88] of the word.

During less festive celebrations, persons with candles may precede the deacon or priest carrying the Book of Gospels from the altar to the ambo during the singing of the Alleluia.[89]

Incense

Since "the use of incense is optional in any form of Mass . . . at the procession and proclamation of the gospel,"[90] it would seem appropriate to use it on Sundays and other festive occasions. Not only the Book of Gospels might be honored with incense, but the entire ambo could be incensed.

Not a Place of Convenience

The ambo, like the altar, is "holy and sacred to this assembly's action and sharing, so it is never used as a table of convenience or as a resting place for papers, notes, . . . or anything else."[91] Only the Book of Gospels or the Lectionary should be placed on the ambo or on a shelf built into it. Of course, both of these books are central and "should be handled and carried in a special way."[92] However, the ambo is also special and should be treated with respect.

Never should loose pages or pamphlets be found on or in the ambo. "The use of pamphlets and leaflets detracts from the visual integrity of the total liturgical action."[93] Furthermore, participation aids can hinder the assembly from seeing, focusing attention on the ambo, and hearing the proclaimer. "The faithful . . . are to listen to the word of God with an inward and outward reverence."[94] They are not to be reading when the Scriptures are being proclaimed. If this is taking place, then worship aids are inhibiting participation and should be discarded. The action of proclaiming and hearing what is proclaimed has no room for every single person to read along. To do this fosters personal devotion but little community worship.

When There Is Need for Another Ambo

If another ambo is needed for the cantor, song leader, commentator, or reader of the announcements, "a very simple lectern, in no way competing or conflicting with the main ambo, and placed for the necessary visibility and audibility, can be used."[95] "It is better for the commentator, cantor, or director of singing . . . not to use the lectern."[96] Nor should the presider use it for any brief announcements before the blessing and dismissal of the Mass. Announcements can be made from the chair by either the deacon, the priest, or from another ambo by another minister.

Conclusion

In general, the reverence shown to the ambo flows from the theology of the word and the theology of the ambo as found in the documents of the Church. The theology of the word and the theology of the ambo should inform praxis, which includes anything that is even remotely near the ambo. In his or her relationship to the ambo, every Christian must remember that "in the readings . . . God is speaking to his people, opening up to them the mystery of redemption and salvation, and nourishing their spirit; Christ is present to the faithful through his own word."[97] The Christian's purpose exists in participating in worship around the assembly's common table of the word of God.

Notes

1. LM, no. 45.
2. Ibid., no. 6.
3. Ibid., no. 21.
4. Ibid., no. 7.
5. BB, no. 1181.
6. BB, no. 1150.
7. Ibid.
8. CSL, no. 35.
9. Ibid., no. 51.
10. Cf. LM, no. 10.
11. LM, no. 47.
12. Ibid.
13. CSL, no. 30.
14. DCCBS.
15. LM, no. 48.
16. EACW, no. 14.
17. LM, no. 3.
18. BB, no. 1181.
19. GIRM, no. 272.
20. LM, no. 32.
21. EACW, no. 74.
22. LM, no. 10.
23. GIRM, no. 34.
24. BB, no. 1182.
25. EACW, no. 74.
26. Ibid.
27. DCA, "Dedication of an Altar," ch. 4, no. 7.
28. LM, no. 4.
29. Ibid.
30. Ibid., no. 5.
31. Ibid., no. 7.
32. EACW, no. 74.
33. DCA:C, 16.
34. DCA, "Dedication of a Church," ch. 2, no. 53.
35. DCA:C, 17.
36. Cf. GIRM, no. 80.
37. GIRM, no. 79.
38. DCA, "Dedication of an Altar," ch. 4, no. 23.
39. Ibid.
40. DCA:C, 17.
41. BB, no. 1175.
42. Ibid., no. 1178.
43. DCA, "Dedication of a Church," ch. 2, no. 31.
44. DCA:C, 30.

45. BB, no. 1181.
46. Ibid.
47. Ibid., no. 1182.
48. Ibid., no. 1183.
49. Ibid., no. 1186.
50. Ibid., no. 1188.
51. Ibid., no. 1189.
52. Ibid., no. 1190.
53. Cf. BB, no. 1191.
54. LM, no. 7.
55. Ibid., no. 32.
56. Ibid., no. 33; cf. GIRM, no. 272.
57. Cf. GIRM, no. 97.
58. Cf. GIRM, no. 99.
59. Cf. GIRM, no. 97; LM, no. 26; EACW, no. 74.
60. Cf. GIRM, no. 99.
61. GIRM, no. 47.
62. LM, no. 31.
63. GIRM, no. 272.
64. DCA, "Dedication of an Altar," ch. 4, no. 6.
65. BB, no. 1173.
66. EACW, no. 73.
67. Ibid.
68. BB, no. 1173.
69. DCA, "Dedication of an Altar," ch. 4, no. 6.
70. EACW, no. 74; cf. BB, no. 1173.
71. LM, no. 34.
72. Ibid., no. 32.
73. Cf. LM, no. 32.
74. EACW, no. 67.
75. LM, no. 32.
76. GIRM, no. 272.
77. LM, no. 34.
78. Ibid., no. 16.
79. Ibid., no. 45.
80. Ibid., no. 52.
81. Ibid., no. 45.
82. Ibid., no. 33.
83. EACW, no. 95.
84. Ibid.
85. Ibid., no. 100.
86. Ibid., no. 71.
87. Cf. EACW, no. 102.
88. EACW, no. 71.
89. Cf. GIRM, no. 94.

90. GIRM, no. 235.
91. EACW, no. 71.
92. Ibid., no. 91.
93. Ibid.
94. LM, no. 45.
95. EACW, no. 75.
96. LM, no. 33; GIRM, no. 272.
97. GIRM, no. 33.

Chapter 4

The Presidential Chair

Ecclesial Documents

The norm of active participation concerning the presidential chair is fleshed out in four documents: (1) the General Instruction of the Roman Missal, (2) *Environment and Art in Catholic Worship,* (3) the rite for the *Dedication of a Church and an Altar,* and (4) the "Order for a Blessing on the Occasion of the Installation of a New Episcopal or Presidential Chair" as found in the *Book of Blessings.*

The "Order for a Blessing on the Occasion of the Installation of a New Episcopal or Presidential Chair" provides introductory words for the presider which encourage the participation of the people: "Let us together, my dear brothers and sisters, praise our God and Lord."[1]

Our consideration here is the theology of the presidential chair found in the documents of the Church and the praxis which should flow from this theology. After exploring the theology of the presidential chair as presented by Vatican Council II, praxis, which either fosters or impedes active participation, will be examined.

It must be noted that the blessing of a presidential chair usually takes place within the rite of a dedication of a church. "When a church is dedicated or blessed, all the appointments that are already in place are considered to be blessed along with the church."[2] However, when "the episcopal chair in the cathedral church and, in other churches, the presidential chair, . . . [is] newly installed or renovated, there is an opportunity to teach the faithful the importance of such [an] appointment by means of the celebra-

73

tion of a blessing."[3] Since the focus is on the presidential chair, only the texts that deal with it will be treated.

Theology of the Presidential Chair

The presidential chair is the chair from where the ordained "presides over the assembly and leads its prayer."[4] "The place for the one who presides, that is, the chair for the priest celebrant, is a symbol of his office of presiding at the liturgical assembly and of guiding the prayer of the people of God."[5] Furthermore, "in the general movement of the liturgical rite, the role of the one who presides is critical and central."[6]

The Cathedra

"The cathedra is the chair from which the bishop of the diocese presides at worship in his cathedral church. One of the most ancient views of the cathedra understands the chair to be the *protokathedra* or seat of the first elder of the Church, an expression of the collegiality of bishops and priests.

At other times in the history of the Church the cathedra was viewed as a throne of a ruling bishop rather than the chair of one who presides in the liturgy."[7] Furthermore, "the chair or *cathedra* of the bishop in the cathedral church is a preeminent sign of the teaching authority belonging to each bishop in his own Church."[8]

It is from the cathedra that the presidential chair in each parish church gets its meaning and importance. Since "it is impossible for the bishop always and everywhere to preside over the whole flock in his church, he must of necessity establish groupings of the faithful; and, among these, parishes, set up locally under a pastor who takes the place of the bishop, are the most important, for in some way they represent the visible Church constituted throughout the world."[9]

For this reason, when a new church is dedicated by the bishop, "the first seating in the chair, even if it is not the object of a particular ritual gesture, has a precise meaning. The bishop, by virtue of his episcopal ordination, in an eminent and visible way acts in the name of Christ teacher, pastor, and pontiff; thus he is first to take the place from which he will preside and exercise the magisterial function. That place, which is simply the chair of the celebrant, is on this occasion a true chair of the bishop."[10]

In parish churches, then, "the priest celebrant's chair ought to stand as a symbol of his office of presiding over the assembly and of directing prayer."[11] However, the presider not only represents the bishop, but he is also a member of the bishop's flock. The chair, therefore, "should be so constructed and arranged" that it is "clearly part of the one assembly, yet conveniently situated for the exercise of [the presider's] respective office."[12] This is not to mean that "the importance of the personal symbol and function of the one who presides in liturgical celebration should . . . be underrated or underplayed, because it is essential for good celebration."[13]

The Order of Blessing a New Presidential Chair

The *Book of Blessings* contains two possibilities in the "Order for a Blessing on the Occasion of the Installation of a New Episcopal or Presidential Chair": the "Order of Blessing Within Mass" and the "Order of Blessing Within a Celebration of the Word of God." The rubrics make it clear that "the rite for the blessing of a new episcopal chair may only be celebrated by the diocesan bishop"[14] or by another bishop delegated by the diocesan bishop. Since the cathedra is the "preeminent sign of the teaching authority belonging to each bishop in his own Church,"[15] it is only proper that the bishop preside at its blessing. Furthermore, any time the bishop visits a parish church he occupies the presidential chair, since the chair on this particular occasion becomes in a sense a cathedra or a visible extension of it.

When the new presidential chair is being blessed in a parish church, it is the bishop's prerogative to preside at the blessing of the chair, since the priest who will occupy it represents the bishop. However, a priest may bless the new or renovated presidential chair.[16]

BLESSING WITHIN MASS

In the "Order of Blessing Within Mass," "on reaching the altar, the celebrant, with the assisting ministers, makes the customary reverence, kisses the altar, and incenses it. Then before going to the episcopal or presidential chair, he signs himself with the sign of the cross."[17] After the greeting, he explains the meaning of the rite being celebrated.

He states that it is "out of his goodness toward us" that our God and Lord "is present through those who are ordained to fulfill a sacred ministry, in order that through them he may teach, sanctify, and shepherd the faithful."[18] The emphasis is placed on the bishop and priests who will preside over the community from the chair. The community is reminded that "every authentic celebration of the eucharist is directed by the bishop, either in person or through the presbyters, who are his helpers."[19] The presider invites the faithful to "ask God to make his servants ever more worthy to carry out such a holy ministry."[20]

A short prayer of blessing addressed to the "Lord Jesus" then follows. The basic theme of the prayer is that the presider is a shepherd of the flock. Like "the Good Shepherd who came to gather [the] scattered sheep into one fold," the bishop and priests have been "chosen as ministers of [the] truth" so that through them Christ can "feed [the] faithful." Furthermore, the bishop and priests are "chosen shepherds" who lead the faithful. The prayer concludes with a petition, which echoes Psalm 23, that the Lord will "one day gather both shepherds and flock into the joyous green pastures of eternity."[21]

Following the prayer of blessing, "the celebrant places incense in the censer and incenses the chair . . . , then takes his place at the chair, where he is incensed by a minister."[22] This ritual action springs from the rite for the *Dedication of a Church and an Altar*. After anointing the altar and the walls of a new church, "a brazier is placed on the altar for burning incense."[23]

"Then the bishop puts incense into some censers and incenses the altar; he returns to the chair, is incensed, and then sits."[24]

"The Book of Revelation (5:8; 8:3-4) says that incense . . . is . . . a symbol of prayer that rises to God."[25] From the chair the presider will direct the prayer of the community.[26] The presider is also incensed in order to emphasize "that the 'temple of God' where we are to offer 'spiritual worship' (Rom 12:1) is the individual baptized Christian."[27] Later, after the gifts of bread and wine have been prepared on the altar, the gifts, the altar, the presider, and all of the people will be incensed[28] in order to emphasize that the "temple of God" is composed of not only individual baptized Christians but, "at the same time, the entire assembly."[29]

The whole church is to be filled "with the fragrance of Christ,"[30] as "all in the assembly gathered for Mass have an individual right and duty to contribute their participation in ways differing according to the diversity of their order and liturgical function. . . . The very arrangement of the celebration itself makes the Church stand out as being formed in a structure of different orders and ministries."[31]

While the presider is incensed "a suitable song is sung,"[32] and then "the Mass, without the penitential rite, continues in the usual manner."[33]

BLESSING WITHIN A CELEBRATION OF THE WORD OF GOD

When the "Order of Blessing Within a Celebration of the Word of God" is used, the rite as outlined above is followed with the exception that the prayer of blessing becomes the opening prayer, which is prayed after the sign of the cross and the introductory remarks. The chair is incensed after the prayer by the presider, and then the presider is incensed by another minister. Choices of two Old Testament readings, two responsorial psalms, and two selections from the Acts of the Apostles are given along with one gospel selection.[34]

Following the homily, in which the presider "gives those present an explanation of the biblical text of Christ's presence in virtue of the fact that ministers act in his name when exercising their office,"[35] are three intercessions. These are introduced with the presider declaring, "Our Lord Jesus Christ so loved the Church that through its ministers and pastors it continues along the path of salvation, taught by the word of God and nourished by the sacraments."[36]

Each of the three intercessions are in the form of a Jewish berakah, or prayer of praise. The first states, "Blessed are you, O Lord, who through the teachers of the faith continue to teach us your Gospel." The second proclaims, "Blessed are you, O Lord, who through the pastors you have chosen continue to feed and strengthen your flock." And the third declares, "Blessed are you, O Lord, who through the heralds of your word continue to urge and exhort us to sing the praises of the Father."[37] It is to be noted that the intercessions highlight the teaching, the sacramental feeding, and the preaching functions of those who preside from the chair.

The prayer of blessing concludes the intercessions. The prayer is addressed to the "Lord Jesus Christ" who "taught the pastors of the Church not to want to be served by others, but to serve." The petition is "that those who preside from this chair will proclaim [the] word ardently and celebrate [the] sacraments rightly, so that, with the people entrusted to their care, they may come before the seat of . . . majesty, there to praise [the Lord] without ceasing."[38] The prayer, obviously, reinforces the themes already stated in the intercessions.

A prayer over the people, which asks God to bless them, to keep them holy and pure, to shower them "with the riches of his glory," to instruct them "with the word of truth, to form their "hearts with the Gospel of salvation," and to enrich them "with love for one another," along with a blessing and a song, concludes the rite.[39]

Praxis

From this understanding of the theology of the presidential chair, there flows a definite practice. As with all the revisions inaugurated by Vatican Council II, the theological background is given as a reason for the praxis which follows.

Only One Presidential Chair

Because "the chair or cathedra of the bishop in the cathedral church is a preeminent sign of the teaching authority belonging to each bishop in his own Church,"[40] "there should be only one cathedra, permanently located in such a way that the bishop is seen really to preside over the entire body of the faithful."[41] This one chair or "cathedra should be especially imposing, because from it the cathedral gets its name and at it the bishop exercises his office as teacher of the faith and presides over the assembly of the faithful."[42]

Likewise, in parish churches there should be but one prominent chair which stands as a symbol of the priest's office of presiding over the assembly and of directing prayer in the place of the bishop.[43] Like the altar, the "symbolic function" of the chair "is rendered negligible" when there are other chairs in sight. "The liturgical space has room for but one."[44]

The chairs for the assisting ministers do not need to be placed on either side of the presidential chair, as this is an arrangement stemming from pre-Vatican II Solemn High Masses when a deacon and subdeacon assisted the presider. The chairs for other ministers should be "conveniently situated for the exercise of their respective offices."[45] However, these chairs do not need to be on either side of the presidential chair.

When a bishop presides in his cathedral church, he occupies the cathedra or presidential chair. "If other bishops or prelates are present, seats should be prepared for them in a suitable place, but not in the form of a cathedra."[46] When a priest presides in the cathedral church, the cathedra is unoccupied. "A seat for the priest who is celebrant should be erected in a different place, but it should always be visible and such as will foster the function of presiding."[47] Therefore, in the cathedral church there will always be two presidential chairs—one which the bishop occupies and one which a priest-presider occupies. The chair for the priest should be proportionally smaller than the cathedra, since it is from the cathedra that this chair receives its meaning and importance.

Placement of the Chair

"The number of steps of the cathedra should be designed in accord with the structure of the individual church building so as to enable the bishop to be seen clearly by the faithful."[48] However, "anything resembling a throne is to be avoided."[49] "The chair . . . should be clearly in a presiding position, although it should not suggest either domination or remoteness."[50] The General Instruction of the Roman Missal suggests that "the best place for the chair is at the back of the sanctuary and turned toward the congregation, unless the structure or other circumstances are an obstacle."[51]

Several points should be noted here. First, arrangements which place the presidential chair against a side wall so that the presider is not facing the assembly should definitely be avoided. Like the altar, the location of the chair "will be central in any eucharistic celebration, but this does not mean it must be spatially in the center or on a central axis. In fact, an off-center location may be a good solution in many cases. Focus and importance in any celebration move with the movement of the rite. Placement and elevation must take into account the necessity of visibility and audibility for all.''[52]

Environment and Art in Catholic Worship clearly states this: "The area of presiding should allow that person to be attentive to and present to the entire congregation, the other ministers, and each part of the liturgical action, even if not personally leading the action at that moment. The place should allow one to conduct the various ministers in their specific activity and roles of leadership, as well as the congregation in its common prayer.''[53]

Second, the presidential chair should be a piece of furniture of "dignity and beauty in materials used, in design and form, in color and texture.''[54] The chair, along with all other furnishings taken together, "should possess a unity and harmony with each other and with the architecture of the place.''[55] This unity and harmony should particularly be seen in the relationship of the chair to the altar and the ambo, since these three pieces of furniture are the most important elements in any worship space.

Third, the presidential chair indeed should be an authentic chair. It "should be not only suitable for its purpose but also capable of making a visual or other sensory contribution to the beauty of the action.''[56] Neither the pre–Vatican II sedilia, a three-part bench with a back, or the scamnum, a bench without arms or back, is a presidential chair. In older churches these pieces of furniture will need to be replaced with a presidential chair. Like the altar, the chair should be "the most beautifully designed and constructed" chair "the community can provide.''[57]

Fourth, unless the back of the chair is placed against the rear of the sanctuary, the chair, like the altar, should stand free and be "approachable from every side, capable of being encircled. It is desirable that candles, cross, any flowers or other decoration in the area should not be so close . . . as to constitute impediments to anyone's approach or movement around" the chair.[58]

Fifth, the presidential chair is not a convenient place for papers, notes, the Sacramentary, song books, or anything else. Book racks or other holders attached to the chair certainly detract from its dignity. If a place is needed to put such items, a small table can be placed next to the chair; on this table can be placed any items needed by the presider.

Presiding from the Chair

In a usual celebration, the presider goes to the chair after approaching the altar, kissing it, and incensing it (if incense is used).[59] "After the entrance song, and with all standing, the priest and the faithful make the sign of the cross. Then, facing the people . . . , the priest greets all present."[60] The penitential rite, the *Kyrie,* the *Gloria,* and the opening prayer are conducted from the chair.[61]

While the Old Testament selection is read, the responsorial psalm sung, and the New Testament reading proclaimed, the presider sits in the chair.[62] If another priest or deacon is to proclaim the gospel, the presider blesses him from the chair.[63] Otherwise, the presider goes to the ambo, where he proclaims the gospel.[64]

If it is to be given, "the priest celebrant gives the homily either at the chair, standing or sitting, or at the lectern."[65] Giving the homily at the chair emphasizes the presider's status as teacher, leader, and sanctifier of the community. It also focuses on the fact that he represents the bishop in the parish, where the priest functions as shepherd of the flock. His authority in the parish is signified by the presidential chair. This authority comes from the bishop, whose cathedra is a sign of his teaching authority in the diocese.

The presider returns to the chair and is seated for a period of silence after the homily.[66] When it is prescribed, the profession of faith is led by the presider while standing at the chair.

"For the general intercessions," which follow the profession of faith, "the celebrant presides at the chair and the intentions are announced at the lectern."[67] By presiding from the chair during the general intercessions, the presider emphasizes his office as director of prayer for the assembly. This sanctifying capacity he received from the bishop when he was entrusted with the care of the people of a particular parish.

When the general intercessions are concluded the presider is seated, while "the servers place the corporal, purificator, chalice, and missal on the altar."[68] Next the presider receives, at the chair, the offerings of the faithful and any other gifts used to meet the needs of the church and of the poor.[69] Then he goes to the altar where the assisting ministers (deacon, server, etc.) have placed the bread and wine, which have been brought forward and received by the presider at the chair.

After Communion "the priest may return to the chair. A period of silence may now be observed, or a hymn of praise or a psalm may be sung."[70] "Then, standing at the altar or at the chair and facing the people, the priest . . . recites the prayer after communion."[71]

From the chair, any brief announcements can be made. These are followed by the greeting and a blessing, which on certain special occasions can be expanded into a solemn blessing or a prayer over the people. Immediately after the blessing, the priest issues the dismissal. He goes to the altar, kisses it, makes the proper reverence with the ministers, and leaves.[72]

Conclusion

In general, the reverence shown to the presidential chair flows from the theology of the presidential chair found in the documents of the Church. The theology of the presidential chair should inform praxis, which includes anything that is directed from the presidential chair. In his or her relationship to the chair, every Christian must remember that "liturgical services . . . are celebrations of the Church which is 'the sacrament of unity,' namely, 'the holy people united and arranged under their bishops,' "[73] who have "received the charge of the community, presiding in God's stead over the flock of which they are the shepherds in that they are teachers of doctrine, ministers of sacred worship and holders of office in government."[74] The Christian's purpose exists in participating in worship around the assembly's shepherd, the man who presiders over and directs the prayer of the assembly from the presidential chair.

Notes

1. BB, nos. 1158 and 1162.
2. Ibid., no. 1150.
3. Ibid.
4. GIRM, no. 60.
5. BB, no. 1154.
6. EACW, no. 60.
7. BCLN 16 (February 1980) 198.
8. BB, no. 1153.
9. CSL, no. 42.
10. DCA:C, 12.
11. GIRM, no. 271.
12. EACW, no. 70.
13. Ibid.
14. BB, no. 1153.
15. Ibid.
16. Ibid., no. 1152.
17. Ibid., no. 1156.
18. Ibid., no. 1158.
19. GIRM, no. 59.

20. BB, no. 1158.
21. Ibid., no. 1159.
22. Ibid., no. 1160.
23. DCA, "Dedication of an Altar," ch. 4, no. 53.
24. Ibid.
25. DCA:C, 29.
26. Cf. GIRM, no. 271.
27. DCA:C, 29–30.
28. Cf. GIRM, no. 235.
29. DCA:C, 30.
30. DCA, "Dedication of an Altar," ch. 4, no. 53.
31. GIRM, no. 58.
32. BB, no. 1160.
33. Ibid., no. 1161.
34. Cf. BB, nos. 1162–67.
35. BB, no. 1168.
36. Ibid., no. 1169.
37. Ibid.
38. Ibid., no. 1170.
39. Ibid., no. 1171; cf. BB, no. 1172.
40. Ibid., no. 1153.
41. BCLN 16 (February 1980) 198.
42. Ibid.
43. Cf. GIRM, no. 271; CSL, no. 42.
44. EACW, no. 72.
45. Ibid., no. 70; cf. GIRM, no. 271.
46. BCLN 16 (February 1980) 198.
47. Ibid.
48. Ibid.
49. GIRM, no. 271.
50. EACW, no. 70.
51. GIRM, no. 271.
52. EACW, no. 73.
53. Ibid., no. 60.
54. Ibid., no. 67.
55. Ibid.
56. Ibid., no. 84.
57. Ibid., no. 71.
58. Ibid.; cf. EACW, no. 89.
59. Cf. GIRM, no. 85.
60. GIRM, no. 86.
61. Cf. GIRM, nos. 87 and 88.
62. Cf. GIRM, no. 89.
63. Cf. GIRM, no. 131.
64. Cf. GIRM, no. 94 and 95.

65. LM, no. 26; cf. GIRM, no. 97.
66. Cf. LM, no. 28.
67. LM, no. 31; cf. GIRM, no. 99.
68. GIRM, no. 100.
69. Cf. GIRM, no. 101.
70. GIRM, no. 121.
71. Ibid., no. 122.
72. Cf. GIRM, nos. 123–25.
73. CSL, no. 26.
74. DCC, no. 20.

Chapter 5

The Tomb and the Womb of the Church

Ecclesial Documents

It is within church buildings that most sacraments are celebrated. "The purpose of the sacraments is to sanctify men [and women], to build up the Body of Christ, and, finally, to give worship to God."[1] Furthermore, "the liturgy of the sacraments . . . sanctifies almost every event of the lives [of the faithful] with the divine grace which flows from the paschal mystery of the Passion, Death and Resurrection of Christ. From this source all sacraments . . . draw their power."[2]

Because sacraments "are signs, they also instruct. . . . By words and objects they . . . nourish, strengthen, and express" faith.[3] Therefore, in order for the sacraments to instruct and nourish faith, people must be actively involved in them in order that they may see how the the paschal mystery is traced in their lives.

The sacrament through which a person is initiated into the paschal mystery and the one associated with the womb of the Church, the font, is baptism. Active participation by all members of the Church is imperative in the celebration of baptism.

This norm of active participation in baptism, in which one is immersed into the paschal mystery, is fleshed out in three documents: (1) "Christian Initiation, General Introduction," found in the *Rite of Baptism for Children* and in the *Rite of Christian Initiation of Adults,* (2) *Environment and Art in Catholic Worship,* and (3) the *Book of Blessings.*

"Christian Initiation, General Introduction" emphasizes that "in the sacraments of Christian initiation we are freed from the power of darkness and joined to Christ's death, burial, and resurrection. We receive the Spirit of filial adoption and are part of the entire people of God."[4] Because "baptism incorporates us into Christ and forms us into God's people,"[5] "the preparation for baptism and Christian instruction are both of vital concern to God's people, the Church, which hands on and nourishes the faith received from the apostles. . . . Therefore it is most important that catechists and other laypersons should work with priests and deacons in the preparation for baptism. In the actual celebration, the people of God should take an active part. Thus they will show their common faith and the shared joy with which the newly baptized are received into the community of the Church."[6]

The *Rite of Baptism for Children* stresses the importance of the community in the celebration of the baptism of both children and adults. "The people of God, that is the Church, made present in the local community, has an important part to play."[7] "Before and after the celebration of the sacrament, the child has a right to the love and help of the community. During the rite . . . , the community exercises its duty when it expresses its assent together with the celebrant after the profession of faith by the parents and godparents. In this way it is clear that the faith in which the children are baptized is not the private possession of the individual family, but it is the common treasure of the whole Church of Christ."[8]

The community should be represented not only by the parents, godparents, and relatives "but, also, . . . by friends, neighbors, and some members of the local Church."[9] However, "parents have a more important ministry and role in the baptism of infants than the godparents."[10]

"Parents, moved by their own faith or with the help of friends or other members of the community, should prepare to take part in the rite with understanding."[11] They, of course, "should be present in the celebration [because] . . . the father and mother have special parts to play. . . . After baptism it is the responsibility of the parents . . . to enable the child to know God."[12]

The *Rite of Christian Initiation of Adults* declares: "The initiation of catechumens is a gradual process that takes place within the community of the faithful. By joining the catechumens in reflecting on the value of the paschal mystery and by renewing their own conversion, the faithful provide an example that will help the catechumens to obey the Holy Spirit more generously."[13]

Furthermore, "the rite of initiation is suited to a spiritual journey of adults that varies according to the many forms of God's grace, the free cooperation of the individuals, the action of the Church, and the circumstance of time and place."[14]

Nowhere is the importance and responsibility of the community more stressed than in this rite: "The people of God, as represented by the local Church, should understand and show by their concern that the initiation of adults is the responsibility of all the baptized."[15] A particular role is assigned to a sponsor, one who "accompanies any candidate seeking admission as a catechumen. Sponsors are persons who have known and assisted the candidates and stand as witnesses to the candidates' moral character, faith, and intention."[16]

Likewise, godparents accompany the candidates. "Godparents are persons chosen by the candidates on the basis of example, good qualities, and friendship, delegated by the local Christian community, and approved by the priest. It is the responsibility of godparents to show the candidates how to practice the Gospel in personal and social life, to sustain the candidates in moments of hesitancy and anxiety, to bear witness, and to guide the candidates' progress in the baptismal life."[17]

In reference to the place of the font, *Environment and Art in Catholic Worship* declares that it "should facilitate full congregational participation."[18] "The entire congregation is an active component. There is no audience, no passive element in the liturgical celebration."[19] The requirements of liturgical celebration and the primary demands that liturgy makes upon the space is "the gathering of the faith community in a participatory and hospitable atmosphere . . . for initiation . . . , for prayer and praise and song."[20]

The "Order for the Blessing of a Baptistery or a New Baptismal Font" in the *Book of Blessings* devotes a whole paragraph to the necessary pastoral preparation for the active participation of the faithful. "The erection of a new baptistery or baptismal font is an important event in the life of a Christian community. The celebration of the blessing should therefore be announced to the faithful well ahead of time and they should be properly prepared to take an active part in the rite. They should be particularly well instructed about the significance of the baptismal font and its sign value, so that they will be inspired with a renewed reverence and appreciation toward baptism and toward the font as a symbol of baptism."[21]

Our consideration here is the theology of the font found in the documents of the Church and the praxis which should flow from this theology and foster active participation. However, in order to understand the theol-

ogy of the font and its praxis, the theology of baptism from which flows the theology of the font and its praxis must first be explored.

Theology of Baptism

Baptism is the first sacrament of a threefold sacramental process, which includes confirmation and Eucharist. Baptism "pardons all our sins, rescues us from the power of darkness, and brings us to the dignity of adopted children, a new creation through water and the Holy Spirit. Hence we are called and are indeed the children of God."[22]

"By signing us with the gift of the Spirit, confirmation makes us more completely the image of the Lord and fills us with the Holy Spirit, so that we may bear witness to him before all the world and work to bring the Body of Christ to its fullness as soon as possible."[23]

"Finally, coming to the table of the eucharist, we eat the flesh and drink the blood of the Son of Man so that we may have eternal life and show forth the unity of God's people. By offering ourselves with Christ, we share in the universal sacrifice, that is, the entire community of the redeemed offered to God by their High Priest, and we pray for a greater outpouring of the Holy Spirit, so that the whole human race may be brought into the unity of God's family.''[24]

Even though ''the three sacraments of Christian initiation closely combine to bring us, the faithful of Christ, to his full stature and to enable us to carry out the mission of the entire people of God in the Church and in the world,''[25] the focus will only be on baptism, ''the first sacrament of the New Law, through which those who firmly accept Christ in faith and receive the Spirit of adoption become in name and fact God's adopted children. Joined with Christ in a death and resurrection like his, they become part of his Body. Filled with the anointing of the Spirit, they become God's holy temple and members of the Church, 'a chosen race, a royal priesthood, a holy nation, God's own people.' ''[26]

Baptism of Children

In the Church there exists the ancient practice of baptizing children and infants as well as adults. ''Children or infants are those who have not yet reached the age of discernment and therefore cannot have or profess personal faith.''[27] However, children ''are baptized in the faith of the Church. This faith is proclaimed for them by their parents and godparents, who represent both the local Church and the whole society of saints and believers.''[28] ''Children must later be formed in the faith in which they have been baptized. Christian formation seeks to lead them gradually to learn God's plan in Christ, so that they may ultimately accept for themselves the faith in which they have been baptized.''[29]

Baptism of Adults

Adults who seek baptism participate in the *Rite of Christian Initiation of Adults,* which ''is designed for adults who, after hearing the mystery of Christ proclaimed, consciously and freely seek the living God and enter the way of faith and conversion as the Holy Spirit opens their hearts.''[30]

Four successive periods make up the initiation of adults: ''the precatechumenate, the period for hearing the first preaching of the Gospel; the period of the catechumenate, set aside for a thorough catechesis . . . ; the period of purification and enlightenment . . . , designed for a more intense spiritual preparation . . . ; and the period of postbaptismal catechesis or mystagogy, marked by the new experience of sacraments and community.''[31]

A Response to the Gospel

In either the case of children or adults, ''baptism is . . . above all, the sacrament of that faith by which, enlightened by the grace of the Holy Spirit, we respond to the Gospel of Christ. That is why the Church believes that it is its most basic and necessary duty to inspire all, catechumens, parents of children still to be baptized, and godparents, to that true and living faith by which they hold fast to Christ and enter into or confirm their commitment to the New Covenant.''[32]

''Baptism is the sacrament by which its recipients are incorporated into the Church and are built up together in the Spirit into a house where God lives.''[33] This leads to worship, as explained in the Dogmatic Constitution on the Church of Vatican Council II: ''Incorporated into the Church by Baptism, the faithful are appointed by their baptismal character to Christian religious worship; reborn as sons [and daughters] of God, they must profess before men [and women] the faith they have received from God through the Church.''[34]

''Baptism is a sacramental bond of unity linking all who have been signed by it.''[35] It ''washes away every stain of sin, original and personal, makes us sharers in God's own life and his adopted children.''[36]

Paschal Character

All of these effects are produced by baptism ''by the power of the mystery of the Lord's passion and resurrection. Those who are baptized are united to Christ in a death like his; buried with him in death, they are given life again with him, and with him they rise again. For baptism recalls and makes present the paschal mystery itself, because in baptism we pass from the death of sin into life.''[37] ''Thus, by Baptism men [and women] are grafted into the paschal mystery of Christ.''[38] ''Through baptism we are formed in the likeness of Christ. . . . In this sacred rite fellowship in Christ's death and resurrection is symbolized and is brought about.''[39]

Therefore, ''the whole initiation must bear a markedly paschal character, since the initiation of Christians is the first sacramental sharing in Christ's dying and rising.''[40] ''The celebration of baptism should reflect the joy of the resurrection.''[41]

The celebration of baptism should also reflect "the connection of baptism with the word of God and with the eucharist, the high point of Christian initiation."[42] In other words, the paschal character of baptism points directly to the threefold sacramental process of baptism, confirmation, and Eucharist.

For this reason, "baptism is a sacramental bond of unity linking all who have been signed by it."[43] It has an "unchangeable effect" and "is held in highest honor by all Christians. Once it has been validly celebrated, even if by Christians with whom we are not in full communion, it may never lawfully be repeated."[44] Baptism incorporates a person into "the entire people of God in the celebration of the memorial of the Lord's death and resurrection."[45]

Therefore, it is best that baptism be celebrated during the Easter Vigil. This is especially true for adults: "The celebration of the sacraments of Christian initiation should take place at the Easter Vigil itself."[46] In the case of infants or children, "to bring out the paschal character of baptism, it is recommended that the sacrament be celebrated during the Easter Vigil or on Sunday, when the Church commemorates the Lord's resurrection."[47]

When there are unusual circumstances or other pastoral needs present such as a large number of persons for baptism, a time other than the Easter Vigil may be chosen. The next choice that is recommended is, obviously, Easter Sunday, followed by a day of the Easter octave or a Sunday during the Easter season.[48]

At other times "as far as possible, the sacraments of initiation are to be celebrated on a Sunday."[49] "On Sunday, baptism may be celebrated . . . during Mass, so that the entire community may be present and the necessary relationship between baptism and eucharist may be clearly seen."[50]

However, whatever day is chosen, "except for a good reason, baptism should not be celebrated more than once on the same day in the same church."[51] This is not merely to avoid the repetition of the rite but to emphasize the community dimension, the participatory aspect, and the paschal character of baptism. "Christ's passover and ours is . . . celebrated. This is given full expression . . . when the Christian initiation of adults is held or at least the baptism of infants."[52]

Theology of the Font

From the theology of baptism flows the theology of the font. The Church does not begin with the font and then construct a theology of baptism.

The Church begins with the theology of baptism and then explains why "the baptistery or site of the baptismal font is rightly considered to be one of the most important parts of a church."[53] The baptistery and font are considered "the womb of the Church" from where "Christians are reborn through water and the Holy Spirit."[54]

"Because baptism is the beginning of the entire Christian life, every cathedral and parish church ought to have its own baptistery or a special place where the baptismal font flows or is situated."[55] So important is this area that "with the consent of the local Ordinary, other churches or chapels may have a baptistery or baptismal font."[56] Moreover, "in the building of a baptistery or in the setting up of a baptismal font the primary consideration must be the proper and worthy celebration of the rites of baptism."[57]

"So that baptism may clearly appear as the sacrament of the Church's faith and of admittance into the people of God, it should normally be celebrated in the parish church, which must have a baptismal font."[58] Therefore, "except in case of danger of death, baptism should not be celebrated in private houses"[59] nor should it be "celebrated in hospitals, except in cases of emergency or for some other pastoral reason of a pressing kind."[60]

Two Types of Baptisteries

In parish churches either of two types of baptisteries may be erected: a place apart from the main body of the church or a place within the main body of the church. "The baptistery may be situated in a chapel either inside or outside the church or in some other part of the church easily seen by the faithful."[61]

"A baptistery separated from the body of the church is to be worthy of the sacrament celebrated there and is to be set aside exclusively for baptism."[62] When the baptistery separated from the main body of the church is not large enough to accomodate a large number of people, "the parts of the rite that are to be celebrated outside the baptistery should be carried out in different areas of the church that most conveniently suit the size of the congregation and the several parts of the baptismal liturgy."[63]

When a baptistery apart from the main body of the church is not possible, then an area "where the baptismal font is located should be reserved for the sacrament of baptism and should be worthy to serve as the place where Christians are reborn in water and the Holy Spirit."[64]

"In the case both of a baptistery that is erected apart from the main body of the church for the celebration of the entire baptismal rite and of a font that is set up within the church itself, everything must be arranged in such a way as to bring out the connection of baptism with the word of God and with the eucharist, the high point of Christian initiation."[65]

Blessing the Baptistery or New Baptismal Font

The best theology of the font is found in the order of blessing the font provided in the Sacramentary during the Easter Vigil and the "Order for the Blessing of a Baptistery or of a New Baptismal Font" found in the *Book of Blessings*. In both rites, no distinction is made between specifically blessing the baptistery or specifically blessing the font. The basic theological understanding of both orders is that the use of the baptistery or font is what in effect blesses it. The end for which the baptistery or font was erected is attained and manifested by the particularly clear signs of water and the baptism of candidates.[66]

Furthermore, "when a church is to be consecrated to God or is to be blessed by use of the rite for the dedication of a church, everything in the church, except the altar, is regarded as blessed and erected in virtue of the rite of dedication or blessing, so that no further rite is needed."[67] However, "when a new baptistery has been erected or a new font installed, it is opportune to celebrate a special rite of blessing."[68]

During the Easter Vigil

The model for the "Order for the Blessing of a Baptistery or of a New Baptismal Font" in the *Book of Blessings* is the liturgy of baptism, the third part of the Easter Vigil. Before looking at the order found in the *Book of Blessings,* the order found in the Easter Vigil will be examined.

Two introductions to the Litany of Saints are provided for the presider in the liturgy of baptism during the Easter Vigil: (1) if there are candidates to be baptized, and (2) if the font is to be blessed but there is no one to be baptized.[69] Both introductions make clear reference to the use of the font. The first introduction says, "As our brothers and sisters approach the waters of rebirth"; the second, "That those reborn in [the font] may be made one with [God's] adopted children in Christ."[70] The invitation to prayer found in the *Rite of Christian Initiation of Adults* likewise places the emphasis on "our brothers and sisters . . . , who are asking for baptism."[71]

LITANY OF SAINTS

If the baptistery is separated from the body of the church, then the Litany of Saints is sung while the Easter candle leads the candidates with their godparents and the presider with the assisting ministers to it.[72] In the Litany two petitions are given to be used, depending on the circumstances. If there are candidates the cantors sing, "Give new life to these chosen ones by the grace of baptism." If there are no candidates but the font is to be blessed, the cantors sing, "By your grace bless this font where your children will be reborn."[73] Again, the reference to the use of the font is what stands out in the Litany of Saints.

The Litany is sung as a reminder that not only those on earth who have already passed from death to life through the waters of baptism and who are about to witness the baptisms of the candidates (or blessing of the font, where baptisms will later take place), but also those who have passed through death to life in baptism and then passed over death to eternal life will witness the initiation of new members immediately (or later). The whole communion of saints is present. A person is baptized into the Church, into the communion of saints. Therefore, the Litany of Saints becomes a special prayer for "those to be born again in baptism."[74]

BLESSING OF WATER

Immediately following the Litany of Saints and its concluding prayer, the water to be used in the baptisms is blessed. The prayer of blessing emphasizes water themes from both the Old Testament and the New Testament. Water is referred to as a "sacramental sign," which tells of the wonders of the Father's unseen power. After stating that water is "a rich symbol of the grace" of baptism, the Old Testament themes of Creation, the Great Flood, and the Exodus through the Red Sea are reinterpreted through the theological lens of baptism.

The New Testament references to Jesus' baptism by John in the Jordan, the Johannine institution of baptism as blood and water flowed from the side of Christ crucified, and the Matthean command to go out and teach all nations and baptize them are employed in the prayer. The presider then prays that the Father will "unseal . . . the fountain of baptism" and "by the power of the Holy Spirit give to the water of this font the grace of [his] Son."[75]

After a reference to the first creation of human beings, the Father is petitioned to now cleanse people "from sin in a new birth of innocence by water and the Spirit.'' Another petition is made for the Father to ''send the Holy Spirit upon the waters of the font'' as the Easter candle may be lowered into the water. The reference to the paschal character of baptism immediately follows:

> May all who are buried with Christ
>   in the death of baptism
>   rise also with him to newness of life.[76]

This prayer of blessing ''declares the religious meaning of water as God's creation and the sacramental use of water in the unfolding of the paschal mystery, and the blessing is also a remembrance of God's wonderful works in the history of salvation.''[77]

''The blessing thus introduces an invocation of the Trinity at the very outset of the celebration of baptism. For it calls to mind the mystery of God's love from the beginning of the world and the creation of the human race; by invoking the Holy Spirit and proclaiming Christ's death and resurrection, it impresses on the mind the newness of Christian baptism, by which we share in his own death and resurrection and receive the holiness of God himself.''[78]

BAPTISMS

Once the water has been blessed adult candidates renounce sin and make the threefold profession of faith in God, the Father, the Son, and the Holy Spirit. Then they are baptized in the name of each Person of the Trinity.[79] The font, now being used for the purpose for which it was created, is blessed in the action of baptizing.

''In their renunciation of sin and profession of faith those to be baptized express their explicit faith in the paschal mystery that has already been recalled in the blessing of water and that will be connoted by the words of the sacrament soon to be spoken by the baptizing minister. Adults are not saved unless they come forward of their own accord and with the will to accept God's gift through their own belief. The faith of those to be baptized is not simply the faith of the Church, but the personal faith of each one of them and each one of them is expected to keep it a living faith.''[80]

The active participation of adult candidates is stressed in the *Rite of Christian Initiation of Adults*.

> Because of the renunciation of sin and the profession of faith . . . the elect will not be baptized merely passively but will receive this great sacrament with

the active resolve to renounce error and to hold fast to God. By their own personal act in the rite of renouncing sin and professing their faith, the elect, as was prefigured in the first covenant with the patriarchs, renounce sin and Satan in order to commit themselves for ever to the promise of the Savior and to the mystery of the Trinity. By professing their faith before the celebrant and the entire community, the elect express the intention, developed to maturity during the preceding periods of initiation, to enter into a new covenant with Christ. Thus these adults embrace the faith that through divine help the Church has handed down, and are baptized in that faith.[81]

The actual baptisms follow the elects' "profession of living faith in Christ's paschal mystery."[82] "In the celebration of baptism the washing with water should take on its full importance as the sign of that mystical sharing in Christ's death and resurrection through which those who believe in his name die to sin and rise to eternal life."[83]

When children are baptized, "faith is proclaimed for them by their parents and godparents, who represent both the local Church and the whole society of saints and believers."[84] Before the parents and godparents renounce sin and profess the Trinitarian faith of the Church, the presider reminds them that they must make it their "constant care" to bring their children up "in the practice of the faith." They are to "see that the divine life which God gives them is kept safe from the poison of sin, to grow always stronger in their hearts." Then, if their faith makes them "ready to accept this responsibility," they renew "the vows" of their "own baptism" by rejecting sin and professing their faith in Christ Jesus. "This is the faith of the Church. This is the faith in which these children are . . . baptized."[85]

ANOINTING WITH CHRISM

If for some serious reason adults are not to be immediately confirmed after baptism, "the celebrant anoints them with chrism immediately after baptism."[86] Likewise, children are anointed "with the chrism of salvation" on the crown of the head.[87] "The anointing with chrism is a sign of the royal priesthood of the baptized and that they are now numbered in the company of the people of God."[88]

Usually, however, "in accord with the ancient practice followed in the Roman liturgy, adults are not to be baptized without receiving confirmation immediately afterward, unless some serious reason stands in the way. The conjunction of the two celebrations signifies the unity of the paschal mystery, the close link between the mission of the Son and the outpouring of the Holy Spirit, and the connection between the two sacraments through which the Son and the Holy Spirit come with the Father to those who are baptized."[89]

CONFIRMATION

The celebration of confirmation begins with a reminder from the presider that those who have just been "born again in Christ by baptism" and have "become members of Christ and of his priestly people" are now "to share in the outpouring of the Holy Spirit . . . , the Spirit sent by the Lord upon his apostles at Pentecost and given by them and their successors to the baptized. The promised strength of the Holy Spirit" will make the newly baptized "more like Christ" and help them "to be witnesses to his suffering, death, and resurrection." It will also strengthen them "to be active members of the Church and to build up the Body of Christ in faith and love."[90]

After an invitation to the entire community to "pray to God . . . to strengthen them with his gifts and anoint them to be more like Christ, the Son of God," the presider prays that the Holy Spirit will be sent upon the sons and daughters freed from sin by water and the Holy Spirit. He concludes:

> Give them the spirit of wisdom and understanding,
> the spirit of right judgment and courage,
> the spirit of knowledge and reverence.
> Fill them with the spirit of wonder and awe in your presence.[91]

Then each person is anointed with chrism on the forehead while the presider says, "N., be sealed with the Gift of the Holy Spirit."[92]

BAPTISMAL GARMENT

After baptism and anointing with chrism (in the case of adults who are not to be confirmed) adults may be clothed by their godparents in a white garment. The accompanying formula said by the presider reminds the newly baptized that they "have become a new creation and have clothed" themselves "in Christ."[93] "The clothing with the baptismal garment signifies the new dignity they have received."[94]

After children have been baptized and chrismated, they receive a white garment as "the outward sign of" their "Christian dignity." With the help of their family and friends "by word and example," they are instructed to bring "that dignity unstained into the everlasting life of heaven."[95]

LIGHT OF CHRIST

Both adults and children are given a lighted candle. In the case of adults "the celebrant takes the Easter candle in his hands or touches it, saying to the godparents: 'Godparents, please come forward to give to the newly baptized the light of Christ.' A godparent of each of the newly baptized goes to the celebrant, lights a candle from the Easter candle, then presents it to the newly baptized."[96]

The newly baptized "have been enlightened by Christ." They are instructed to "walk always as children of the light and [to] keep the flame of faith alive" in their hearts.[97] Just as Christ was proclaimed to be the light at the beginning of the Easter Vigil, the newly baptized are smaller lights. "The presentation of the lighted candle shows that they are called to walk as befits the children of the light."[98]

When children are baptized, "the celebrant takes the Easter candle and says: Receive the light of Christ. Someone from the family lights the child's candle from the Easter candle."[99] The instruction is then given to the parents and godparents. The child, who is referred to as "this light" is entrusted to them "to be kept burning brightly." They have "been enlightened by Christ. They are to walk always as children of the light." With the help of the parents and godparents, the children will be able "to keep the flame of faith alive in their hearts."[100]

EPHPHETHA

For adults, the ephphetha rite, or rite of opening the ears and mouth, may be celebrated with the elect sometime on Holy Saturday as immediate preparation for the sacraments of initiation. After a proclamation of Mark 7:31-37, the scriptural basis for the rite, and a brief explanation of the text, the celebrant touches the right and left ear of each and the closed lips of each of the elect with his thumb and says the following formulary:

> Ephphetha: that is, be opened,
> that you may profess the faith you hear,
> to the praise and glory of God.[101]

"By the power of its symbolism the ephphetha . . . impresses on the elect their need of grace in order that they may hear the word of God and profess it for their salvation."[102]

In the rite of baptizing children, after the presentation of the lighted candle this rite is performed at the discretion of the presider. As he touches the ears and mouth of each child with his thumb, he says: "The Lord Jesus made the deaf hear and the dumb speak. May he soon touch your ears to receive his word, and your mouth to proclaim his faith, to the praise and glory of God the Father."[103]

RENEWAL OF BAPTISMAL PROMISES

"When the rite of baptism (and confirmation) has been completed . . . all present stand with lighted candles and renew their baptismal profession of faith."[104] The presider reminds the faithful that "through the paschal mystery" they "have been buried with Christ in baptism," so that they "may rise with him to a new life."[105] After renouncing sin and professing their faith in the Trinity, the people are sprinkled with the blessed water from the baptismal font while a song which is baptismal in character is sung.[106] "In this way the gestures and words recall to [the faithful] the baptism they have received."[107] "Meanwhile the newly baptized are led to their place among the faithful."[108]

BLESSING OF WATER IF THERE ARE NO BAPTISMS

"If no one is to be baptized and the font is not to be blessed during the Easter Vigil, the priest blesses . . . water," which will be used "to recall . . . baptism."[109] The prayer of blessing is one of recollection of "the wonder of . . . creation and the greater wonder of . . . redemption."[110] Some of the same themes found in the blessing of water when there are candidates for baptism or when the font is to blessed are reiterated. The focus of the prayer, however, is on the community as the presider asks God to let the "water remind [all] of . . . baptism," and to let all "share the joys of . . . brothers [and sisters] who are baptized this Easter."[111]

This is not the preferred rite at the Easter Vigil but one which would have to be employed in the case when there are no candidates for baptism and when the font is not to be blessed.[112] The passover of Christ "is given full expression in those churches which have a baptismal font and more so when the Christian initiation of adults is held or at least the baptism of infants." But, "even if there are no candidates for baptism, the blessing of baptismal water should still take place in parish churches. If this blessing does not take place at the baptismal font but in the sanctuary, baptismal water should be carried afterward to the baptistery, there to be kept throughout the whole of paschal time."[113]

"The water blessed at the Easter Vigil should, if possible, be kept and used throughout the Easter season to signify more clearly the relationship between the sacrament of baptism and the paschal mystery. Outside the Easter season, it is desirable that the water be blessed for each occasion, in order that the words of blessing may explicitly express the mystery of salvation that the Church remembers and proclaims."[114]

Blessing a New Baptistery or New Baptismal Font at Other Times

Since it is possible to bless the baptismal font during the Easter Vigil, this yearly celebration would seem to eliminate the need for a separate blessing of a baptistery or baptismal font. However, "when a new baptistery has been erected or a new font installed, it is opportune to celebrate a special rite of blessing."[115] Because "the reception of baptism stands as the beginning of the faithful's life in Christ that in some way derives from and depends on their high priest, the bishop, in his own diocese the bishop himself . . . should dedicate a new baptistery or new baptismal font."[116]

"As a rule the day designated for the celebration of the blessing should be a Sunday, especially a Sunday of the Easter season or the Sunday or feast of the Baptism of the Lord, in order to bring out more clearly the paschal character of baptism and to make possible a large attendance of the faithful."[117]

Two orders for blessing the baptismal font are given. The first is the blessing with the celebration of baptism, and the second is without the celebration of baptism.

BLESSING THE FONT WITH BAPTISMS

When baptism is to be celebrated with the blessing of a new baptismal font, the presider and other ministers "proceed from the sacristy through the body of the church to the baptistery; they are led by a censer bearer carrying a censer with lighted charcoal; they are followed by an acolyte bearing the Easter candle and by other persons in the procession" along with the candidates for baptism and their sponsors.[118] During the procession the Litany of Saints is sung as during the Easter Vigil.[119]

When the procession reaches the baptistery, "the Easter candle is placed on the candlestand prepared for it at the center of the baptistery or near the font."[120] When the Litany of Saints has ended, the presider greets the assembly in the usual way; then he "prepares those present for the blessing."[121]

The emphasis of the explanation is on the use that will be made of the font for baptism. "We are about to bless a new baptismal font and to bestow on these elect the sacrament of their rebirth. . . . They will . . . become members of a people set apart, the Church; they will be joined to Christ, the firstborn of many brothers and sisters, and, having received the Holy Spirit of adoption, they will dare to call upon God as Father in virtue of being his children."[122]

The opening prayer immediately follows. This prayer again makes reference to those "who will come forth reborn from [the] saving font" and echoes the womb-of-the-Church theme by referring to the Church as "their mother."[123]

Those who are to be baptized are then welcomed according to the *Rite of Christian Initiation of Adults* or the *Rite of Baptism for Children*. The Liturgy of the Word follows, after which "the celebrant in the homily explains the biblical texts, so that those present may better understand the importance of baptism and the symbolism of the font."[124] The homily is followed by the rites which precede baptism.

Then "the candidates gather around the font, the infants held by their mothers and the adults standing with their godparents."[125] The presider invites the faithful to pray. "Through the prayer of the Church," he states, "the gift of the Holy Spirit will endow" the waters of the font "with the power to sanctify." First, however, prayers are offered to God for his servants "who are asking to be baptized."[126] The prayer of blessing for the font follows the invitation.

PRAYER OF BLESSING THE NEW FONT

In the prayer of blessing of the new font, the presider praises the "Lord God, Creator of the world and Father of all who are born into it," for allowing those present to "open this saving font through the liturgy of [the] Church."[127] Here, it is important to notice that it is through the liturgy—the official, public, ritual, formal worship of the Church—that the new font becomes effective.

"Here the door is reopened to the life of the spirit," declares the presider, "and the gateway to the Church is swung wide to those against whom the gates of paradise were shut."[128] By being immersed in the font, a person is baptized in water and the Spirit, and the primordial "Genesis" gate is now reopened to a pathway that leads through the Church.

The rest of the prayer echoes biblical references to water; in this regard it is similar to the prayer of blessing the water found in the liturgy of baptism of the Easter Vigil.

The first reference is to the Johannine account of the healing near the pool of Bethesda.[129] The presider prays,

> This pool is opened and in it the newness of its pure waters
> will again make clean and spotless
> those who were stained by the old ways of sin.[130]

The second reference is to the Great Flood. "A new torrent is released whose gushing waters sweep away sin and bring new virtue to life."[131]

Two Johannine echoes are found in the next part of the prayer. The first is to the words of Jesus on the last and greatest day of the feast of Tabernacles,[132] and the second is to the last event on the cross before Jesus is taken down and placed in the tomb.[133]

> A stream of living water, coming from Christ's side, now flows
> and those who drink this water will be brought to eternal life.[134]

The fourth reference refers to the pillar of fire, which led the Israelites through the Exodus,[135] and the Easter candle, which represents the new leader, Jesus, who leads his people through death to the passover to new life through the waters of baptism.[136]

> Over this font the lamp of faith spreads the holy light
> that banishes darkness from the mind
> and fills those who are reborn here with heavenly gifts.[137]

In Paul's Letter to the Romans, he speaks about being buried with Christ through baptism.[138] This particular section of the letter (ch. 6) forms the epistle for the Easter Vigil. The prayer of blessing echoes this burial-through-baptism theme:

> Those who profess their faith at this font
> are plunged beneath the waters and joined to Christ's death,
> so that they may rise with him to newness of life.[139]

The prayer of blessing turns from praise to petition to the Lord

> . . . to send the life-giving presence of [the] Spirit upon this font,
> placed here as the source of new life for . . . people.[140]

Then follows the sixth scriptural reference.

The incarnation is echoed when the presider prays, "The power of the Spirit made the Virgin Mary the mother of [God's] Son."[141] Since the font is the womb of the Church, the mother of all God's children, the presider prays that God will

> send forth the power of the same Spirit,
> so that [the] Church may present [God]
> with countless new sons and daughters
> and bring forth new citizens of heaven.[142]

This leads directly to the last part of the prayer, which is for "the people who are reborn from this font." The presider prays that they

> may fulfill in their actions
> what they pledge by their faith
> and show by their lives
> what they begin by the power of [God's] grace.
> [That] the people of different nations and conditions
> who come forth as one from these waters of rebirth
> show by their love that they are brothers and sisters
> and by their concord that they are citizens of the one kingdom.
> [That all be made] into true sons and daughters
> who reflect their Father's goodness,
> disciples who are faithful to the teaching of their one Master,
> temples in whom the voice of the Spirit resounds
> . . . that they may be witnesses to the Gospel,
> doers of the works of holiness.
> [And that they may] fill with the Spirit of Christ
> the earthly city where they live,
> until they are welcomed home in the heavenly Jerusalem.[143]

When the prayer of blessing is complete, "the celebrant places incense in the censer and incenses the font."[144] "Fire recalls the Holy Spirit, that fire sent upon the Church by Christ, risen and seated at [the] Father's right hand (see Acts 2:1-3)."[145] This ritual also suggests "that the 'temple of God' where we are to offer 'spiritual worship' (Rom 12:1) is the individual baptized Christian."[146]

BAPTISMS

Children are baptized according to the *Rite of Baptism for Children* and adults according to the *Rite of Christian Initiation of Adults*.[147] "In accord with ancient tradition, at the Christian initiation of adults, after baptism, the newly baptized receive the sacrament of confirmation and for the first time participate in the eucharist."[148]

BLESSING THE FONT WITHOUT BAPTISMS

When a new font is to be blessed but there are no candidates for baptism, the "Order of Blessing of a New Baptismal Font Without the Celebration of Baptism" is followed. The procession to the baptistery takes place as outlined above, along with the greeting by the presider and the instruction, which prepares those present for the blessing. The instruction differs only in that the reference to those about to be baptized is removed. The wording points to the future, to those "who will come forth reborn" from the new font.[149]

This future-oriented theme is also found in the prayer, which follows. The presider prays:

> O God,
> by the sacrament of rebirth
> you continually increase the number of your children.
> Grant that all who will come forth from this saving font
> may by their way of life give glory to your name
> and add to the holiness of the Church, their mother.[150]

The Liturgy of the Word follows. The readings are chosen from the Lectionary from either the celebration of "Christian Initiation Apart from the Easter Vigil" or for the "Baptism of Children."[151] The homily "explains the biblical texts, so that those present may better understand the importance of baptism and the symbolism of the font."[152]

PRAYER OF BLESSING THE NEW FONT

The prayer of blessing of the new font is exactly as that given when baptism is to be celebrated. The only part that differs is the invitation to prayer. Instead of inviting those present to pray for those "who are asking to be baptized,"[153] the presider instructs the faithful to "first pray to God our Father that he will keep the faith alive in our community and increase the bonds of love between us." He continues, "For the font of baptism is truly opened when our ears are heedful of God's word; when our minds are brightened with Christ's light and closed to the darkness of sin; when our hearts are bound closely to the Lord and renounce Satan and all his works."[154] Obviously the focus of prayer is on the community that is present.

"After the invocation over the font, the celebrant places incense in the censer and incenses the font; during this time, a baptismal song may be sung."[155] Then, "all may renew their profession of baptismal faith."[156]

RENEWAL OF BAPTISM

The members of the congregation are instructed by the presider to "call to mind . . . the faith . . . professed when [they] received the sacraments of Christian initiation, so that, led by the grace of the Holy Spirit, [they] may have the power to live up to it more fully each day."[157] All present are questioned as at the Easter Vigil and as on Easter Sunday. The presider assents to the profession of faith by proclaiming: "This is our faith. This is the faith of the Church. We are proud to profess it in Christ Jesus our Lord."[158] "Then the celebrant takes the sprinkler and sprinkles the assembly with water from the newly blessed font."[159]

GENERAL INTERCESSIONS

The intercessions stress the paschal character of baptism. The presider introduces them by saying, "Through the paschal mystery our loving Father has given us rebirth from water and the Holy Spirit into a new life as his own children."[160]

Five petitions echo biblical references. The first is to creation: "Father of mercies, you have created us in your own image and sanctified us through baptism; make us always and everywhere conscious of your gift and of our Christian dignity."[161]

The second is from the Gospel of John: "From the side of Christ you brought forth the waters of the Holy Spirit; make this life-giving water that we receive become for us a fountain of living water leaping up to provide eternal life."[162]

The third petition refers to the First Letter of Peter: "In the waters of baptism you have made us a chosen race, a royal priesthood, a holy people; grant that we will fulfill our Christian responsibilities by proclaiming your goodness to all."[163]

The fourth and fifth petitions are for those to be "reborn in the water of this font." All pray that they "will live up to what they have acknowledged in faith," and that catechumens will discover the newly erected font to be "the pool of new life."[164] Finally, the font serves as "a reminder of constant renewal of life" for all.[165]

The intercessions are followed by the recitation of the Lord's Prayer. The presider concludes with a prayer that echoes Paul's baptism-into-the-death-of-Christ theme in his Letter to the Romans. The presider prays:

O God,
who endowed these waters with the power of death and life,
grant that those who are buried with Christ in this font
may put aside all sin
and rise again with him,
clothed in the radiant garment of immortality.[166]

A blessing is to be followed by "a song expressing paschal joy and thanksgiving."[167] Then the people are dismissed.[168]

Praxis

From this understanding of the theology of baptism and the theology of the font, there flows a definite practice. As with all the revisions inaugurated by Vatican Council II, the theological background is given as a reason for the praxis which follows.

The Font

In the baptistery the most important item is the font, which "should be stationery."[169] The permanent font in the baptistery is not to be confused with "the vessel in which on occasion the water is prepared for the sacrament in the sanctuary."[170] The "Order for the Blessing of a Baptistery or of a New Baptismal Font" "is not celebrated"[171] "in the case simply of a portable vessel."[172]

Because "immersion is the fuller and more appropriate symbolic action in baptism," in the case of fonts which "are not so constructed [to allow for immersion], the use of a portable one is recommended."[173] "When a portable font is used, it should be placed for maximum visibility and audibility, without crowding or obscuring the altar, ambo and chair."[174]

The place of the stationary font, "whether it is in an area near the main entrance of the liturgical space or one in the midst of the congregation, should facilitate full congregational participation, regularly in the Easter Vigil."[175]

The font should be large enough to facilitate immersion, "which is more suitable as a symbol of participation in the death and resurrection of Christ."[176] "New baptismal fonts . . . should be constructed to allow for the immersion of infants, at least, and to allow for the pouring of water over the entire body of a child or adult."[177]

When a new baptismal font is constructed, the "dignity and beauty in materials used, in design and form, in color and texture" must be considered.[178] Likewise, the font with "all furnishings taken together should possess a unity and harmony . . . with the architecture of the place."[179] It should be "gracefully constructed out of a suitable material, of splendid beauty and spotless cleanliness."[180]

"In order to enhance its force as a sign, the font should be designed in such a way that it functions as a fountain of running water."[181] "If the baptismal space is in a gathering place or entry way, it can have living, moving water."[182] "If the baptistery is supplied with running water, the blessing [of the water] is given as the water flows."[183]

It is important to note, however, that "the water used in baptism should be true water and, both for the sake of authentic sacramental symbolism, and for hygienic reasons, should be pure and clean."[184]

When flowing water is available, "provision for warming the water for immersion" should be made.[185] When running water is not available and "if the climate requires, provision should be made for the water to be heated beforehand."[186]

Other Items

Besides the font with its requirements, "for celebrating the liturgy of the word of God a suitable place should be provided in the baptistery or in the church."[187] In fact, "everything must be arranged in such a way as to bring out the connection of baptism with the word of God and with the eucharist, the high point of Christian initiation."[188]

There should also be room for the Easter candle and its stand, which after the Easter season "should be kept reverently in the baptistery, in such a way that it can be lighted for the celebration of baptism and so that from it the candles for the newly baptized can easily be lighted."[189] It should be located either "at the center of the baptistery or near the font."[190]

The baptistery itself "should be large enough to accommodate a good number of people."[191] If it is not large, then "in the celebration the parts of the rite that are to be celebrated outside the baptistery should be carried out in different areas of the church that most conveniently suit the size of the congregation and the several parts of the baptismal liturgy." "When the baptistery cannot accommodate all the catechumens and the congregation, the parts of the rite that are customarily celebrated inside the baptistery may be transferred to some other suitable area of the church."[192]

Conclusion

In general, the reverence shown to the font flows from the theology of baptism and the theology of the font as found in the documents of the Church. The theology of baptism and the theology of the font should inform praxis.

Every Christian must pass through the waters of the font. When this is done the whole community celebrates death and resurrection. The Christian's purpose exists in participating in worship around the assembly's common source of death and life, its tomb and womb, the baptismal font.

Notes

1. CSL, no. 59.
2. Ibid., no. 61.
3. Ibid., no. 59.
4. CIGI, no. 1.
5. Ibid., no. 2.
6. Ibid., no. 7.
7. RBC, no. 4.
8. Ibid.
9. CIGI, no. 7.
10. RBC, no. 5.
11. Ibid.
12. Ibid.
13. RCIA, no. 4.
14. Ibid., no. 5.
15. Ibid., no. 9.
16. Ibid., no. 10.
17. Ibid., no. 11.
18. Ibid., no. 77.
19. Ibid., no. 30.
20. Ibid., no. 40.
21. BB, no. 1089.
22. CIGI, no. 2.
23. Ibid.
24. Ibid.
25. Ibid.
26. BB, no. 1080.
27. RBC, no. 1.
28. Ibid., no. 2.
29. Ibid., no. 3.
30. RCIA, no. 1.

31. Ibid., no. 7.
32. CIGI, no. 3.
33. Ibid., no. 4.
34. DCC, no. 11.
35. CIGI, no. 4.
36. CIGI, no. 5.
37. CIGI, no. 6.
38. CSL, no. 6.
39. DCC, no. 7.
40. RCIA, no. 8; cf. CIGI, no. 28.
41. CIGI, no. 6.
42. BB, no. 1083.
43. CIGI, no. 4.
44. Ibid.
45. Ibid., no. 1.
46. RCIA, no. 23; cf. RCIA, no. 26.
47. RBC, no. 9.
48. Cf. RCIA, nos. 23 and 26.
49. RCIA, no. 27.
50. RBC, no. 9.
51. CIGI, no. 27.
52. PCPF, no. 88.
53. BB, no. 1080.
54. Ibid., no. 1084.
55. Ibid., no. 1081; cf. CCL, 858:1.
56. Ibid.; cf. RBC, no. 11; cf. CCL, 858:2.
57. BB, no. 1082.
58. RBC, no. 10.
59. Ibid., no. 12.
60. Ibid., no. 13.
61. CIGI, no. 25.
62. BB, no. 1084.
63. CIGI, no. 26.
64. Ibid., no. 25.
65. BB, no. 1083.
66. Cf. DCA, "Dedication of an Altar," ch. 4, no. 23.
67. BB, no. 1078; cf. BB, no. 1150.
68. BB, no. 1086.
69. Cf. TS, The Easter Vigil, no. 38.
70. Ibid.
71. RCIA, no. 220.
72. Cf. TS, The Easter Vigil, no. 39.
73. TS, The Easter Vigil, no. 41.
74. Ibid.
75. Ibid., no. 42.

76. Ibid.
77. RCIA, no. 210.
78. Ibid.
79. Cf. RCIA, nos. 223–26.
80. RCIA, no. 211.
81. Ibid.
82. Ibid., no. 212.
83. Ibid., no. 213.
84. RBC, no. 2.
85. Ibid., no. 56.
86. RCIA, no. 228.
87. RBC, no. 62.
88. RCIA, no. 214.
89. Ibid., no. 215.
90. Ibid., no. 233.
91. Ibid., nos. 233–34.
92. Ibid., no. 235.
93. Ibid., no. 229.
94. Ibid., no. 214.
95. RBC, no. 63.
96. RCIA, no. 230.
97. Ibid.
98. Ibid., no. 214.
99. RBC, no. 64.
100. Ibid.
101. RCIA, no. 199.
102. Ibid., no. 197.
103. RBC, no. 65.
104. TS, The Easter Vigil, no. 46; cf. RCIA, no. 237.
105. Ibid.
106. Ibid., no. 47.
107. PCPF, no. 89.
108. TS, The Easter Vigil, no. 48.
109. Ibid., no. 45.
110. Ibid.
111. Ibid.
112. Cf. PCPF, no. 88.
113. PCPF, no. 88.
114. CIGI, no. 21.
115. BB, no. 1086.
116. Ibid., no. 1087.
117. Ibid., no. 1088.
118. Ibid., no. 1092.
119. Cf. BB, no. 1093.
120. BB, no. 1094.

121. Ibid., no. 1095.
122. Ibid.
123. Ibid., no. 1096.
124. Ibid., no. 1099.
125. Ibid., no. 1011.
126. Ibid.
127. Ibid.
128. Ibid.
129. Cf. John 5:1-9.
130. BB, no. 1101.
131. Ibid.
132. Cf. John 7:37-39.
133. Cf. John 19:34.
134. BB, no. 1101.
135. Cf. Exod 13:22.
136. TS, The Easter Vigil, no. 18.
137. BB, no. 1101.
138. Cf. Rom 6:3-4.
139. BB, no. 1101.
140. Ibid.
141. Ibid.
142. Ibid.
143. Ibid.
144. Ibid., no. 1102.
145. DCA:C, 29.
146. Ibid., 29–30.
147. Cf. BB, no. 1103.
148. BB, no. 1108.
149. Ibid., no. 1112.
150. Ibid., no. 1113.
151. Cf. BB, no. 1114.
152. BB, no. 1115.
153. Ibid., no. 1101.
154. Ibid., no. 1116.
155. Ibid., no. 1118.
156. Ibid., no. 1119.
157. Ibid.
158. Ibid.
159. Ibid., no. 1120.
160. Ibid., no. 1121
161. Ibid.
162. Ibid.
163. Ibid.
164. Ibid.
165. Ibid.

166. Ibid., no. 1122.
167. Ibid., no. 1123.
168. Cf. BB, no. 1124.
169. BB, no. 1085.
170. CIGI, no. 19.
171. BB, no. 1086.
172. Ibid.
173. EACW, no. 76.
174. Ibid., no. 77.
175. Ibid.
176. CIGI, no. 22.
177. EACW, no. 76; cf. BB, no. 1085.
178. EACW, no. 67.
179. Ibid.
180. BB, no. 1085; cf. CIGI, no. 19.
181. BB, no. 1085.
182. EACW, no. 77.
183. CIGI, no. 21.
184. Ibid., no. 18.
185. EACW, no. 77.
186. CIGI, no. 20; cf. BB, no. 1085.
187. CIGI, no. 24.
188. BB, no. 1083.
189. CIGI, no. 25; cf. BB, no. 1094.
190. BB, nos. 1094 and 1111.
191. CIGI, no. 25.
192. Ibid., no. 26.

Chapter 6

The Tabernacle and Eucharistic Reservation

Ecclesial Documents

The norm of active participation concerning the reserved Eucharist is fleshed out in six documents: (1) the General Instruction of the Roman Missal, (2) "Holy Communion and Worship of the Eucharist Outside of Mass," (3) the Instruction on the Worship of the Eucharistic Mystery, (4) *Environment and Art in Catholic Worship*, (5) the *Book of Blessings*, and (6) the rite for the *Dedication of a Church and an Altar*.

The General Instruction of the Roman Missal encourages the active participation of the faithful in adoration and prayer: "Every encouragement should be given to the practice of eucharistic reservation in a chapel suited to the faithful's private devotion and prayer."[1]

"Holy Communion and Worship of the Eucharist Outside of Mass" states: "The place for the reservation of the eucharist should be truly preeminent. It is highly recommended that the place be suitable also for private adoration and prayer so that the faithful may easily, fruitfully, and constantly honor the Lord, present in the sacrament, through personal worship."[2]

The Instruction on the Worship of the Eucharistic Mystery points out that

> the primary and original purpose of the reserving of the sacred species in church outside Mass is the administration of the Viaticum. Secondary ends are the distribution of communion outside Mass and the adoration of Our Lord Jesus Christ concealed beneath these same species. . . . The reservation of the sa-

113

cred species for the sick . . . led to the praiseworthy custom of adoring the
heavenly food which is preserved in churches. This practice of adoration has
a valid and firm foundation, especially since belief in the real presence of the
Lord has as its natural consequence the external and public manifestation of
that belief.[3]

This document then declares that "the devotion which leads the faithful
to visit the Blessed Sacrament draws them into an ever deeper participation
in the Paschal Mystery."[4]

Environment and Art in Catholic Worship declares, "Beyond the celebration of the eucharist, the Church has had a most ancient tradition of reserving
the eucharistic bread."[5] After restating the purpose of reservation, "to bring
communion to the sick and to be the object of private devotion,"[6] this
document states: "Most appropriately, this reservation should be designated
in a space designed for individual devotion. . . . A space carefully designed

and appointed can give proper attention to the reserved sacrament."[7] The space should "support private meditation without distractions."[8]

The "Order for the Blessing of a New Tabernacle" in the *Book of Blessings* encourages active participation in the worship of the Lord present in the reserved species. After recalling that "the tabernacle . . . is a reminder of Christ's presence . . . ," the introduction to the blessing states that "it is also a reminder of the brothers and sisters we must cherish in charity, since it was in fulfillment of the sacramental ministry received from Christ that the Church first began to reserve the eucharist for the sake of the sick and the dying. In our churches adoration has always been offered to the reserved sacrament."[9]

When a new church is dedicated, one of the rites is the "Inauguration of the Blessed Sacrament Chapel." This is the place "where the blessed sacrament is to be reserved."[10] "The fruitful participation of the people"[11] in all of the rites of dedication is emphasized.

Our consideration here is the theology of the tabernacle found in the documents of the Church and the praxis which should flow from this theology and foster active participation. However, in order to understand the theology of the tabernacle and its praxis, the theology of the Eucharist must first be explored. It is from the theology of the Eucharist that the theology of the tabernacle and its praxis flows.

Theology of Eucharist

The General Introduction to "Holy Communion and Worship of the Eucharist Outside of Mass" emphasizes, "The celebration of the eucharist in the sacrifice of the Mass is truly the origin and the goal of the worship which is shown to the eucharist outside Mass."[12] Also, the Instruction on the Worship of the Eucharistic Mystery states that "the celebration of the eucharist is the true center of the whole Christian life both for the universal Church and for the local congregation of that Church."[13]

This "true center" consists of active participation. "The *celebration* of the eucharist is the focus of the normal Sunday assembly. As such, the major space of a church is designed for this *action.*"[14] "The sacred species, the body and blood of the Lord, are on the altar to be distributed as food and drink to the faithful."[15]

However, "beyond the celebration of the eucharist, the Church has had a most ancient tradition of reserving the eucharistic bread."[16] "It is not the presence of the reserved sacrament that makes the church 'sacred' and makes of it a *domus Dei* in the genuine sense of the word; nonetheless, the reservation of the blessed sacrament is a precious good for the spiritual life of the community."[17]

With this emphasis on the centrality of the celebration of the Eucharist, there emerges the purpose of reserving the Eucharistic species, namely for "the administration of the Viaticum. Secondary ends are the distribution of communion outside Mass and the adoration of Our Lord Jesus Christ concealed beneath these same species."[18]

Reservation Is Secondary to Celebration

The documents of the Church make the celebration of the Eucharist a priority, and they demonstrate how the reservation of the Eucharist is secondary to the celebration of the Eucharist. "Therefore, to express the sign of the eucharist, it is more in harmony with the nature of the celebration that, at the altar where Mass is celebrated, there should if possible be no reservation of the sacrament in the tabernacle from the beginning of Mass. The eucharistic presence of Christ is the fruit of the consecration and should appear to be such."[19]

This directive is in keeping with the rubrics which are given for the Evening Mass of the Lord's Supper on Holy Thursday: "The tabernacle should be entirely empty; a sufficient amount of bread should be consecrated at this Mass for the communion of clergy and laity today and tomorrow."[20]

Exposition

Furthermore, in order to demonstrate that "the sacrifice of the Mass is truly the origin and the goal of the worship which is shown to the eucharist outside Mass,"[21] during periods of exposition of the Eucharist the host used for exposition "should be consecrated in the Mass which immediately precedes the exposition and after communion should be placed in the monstrance upon the altar."[22] To further emphasize this point, "during the exposition of the blessed sacrament, the celebration of Mass is prohibited in the body of the Church."[23]

The reservation and the exposition of the Eucharist "must clearly express the cult of the blessed sacrament in its relationship to the Mass" and "carefully avoid anything which might somehow obscure the principal desire of Christ in instituting the eucharist, namely, to be with us as food, medicine, and comfort."[24]

All Actively Share in One Eucharist

This understanding is emphasized in the General Instruction of the Roman Missal. "The eucharistic bread should be made in such a way that in a Mass with a congregation the priest is able to actually break the host into parts and distribute them to at least some of the faithful."[25] Likewise, the Instruction on the Worship of the Eucharistic Mystery states, "In order that, even through signs, the communion may be seen more clearly to be participation in the sacrifice which is being celebrated, care should be taken to enable the faithful to communicate with hosts consecrated during the Mass."[26]

The practice of receiving the Eucharistic wine by drinking from the cup is another attempt to emphasize the celebration and participatory aspect of the faithful in the Mass.

The Instruction on the Worship of the Eucharistic Mystery declares: "The celebration of the Eucharist . . . is the action not only of Christ, but also of the Church. . . . The Church, the spouse and minister of Christ, performs together with him the role of priest and victim, offers him to the Father and at the same time makes a total offering of herself together with him."[27] The Eucharist, "the memorial of the Lord, . . . signifies and effects the unity of all who believe in him."[28]

"The more clearly the faithful understand the place they occupy in the liturgical community and the part they have to play in the eucharistic action, the more conscious and fruitful will be the active participation which is proper to that community."[29]

Emphasis Placed on Celebration

To further emphasize the active celebration aspect over the passive reservation aspect of the Eucharist, the General Introduction to "Holy Communion and Worship of the Eucharist Outside of Mass" highly recommends that the place where the tabernacle is located be in a "chapel . . . separate from the body of the church"[30] because "the major space of a church is designed for . . . action."[31]

Therefore, "the general plan of the sacred building should be such that it reflects in some way the whole assembly. It should allow for the distribution of all in due order and facilitate each one's proper function."[32]

Theology of the Tabernacle

The theology of active participation in the Eucharistic celebration is enfleshed in the rite for the "Inauguration of a Blessed Sacrament Chapel During the Dedication of a New Church." This particular rite emphasizes that "the place of reservation is inaugurated by using it."[33]

Inauguration of a Blessed Sacrament Chapel

The rite takes place after the Communion of the faithful during the dedication ceremony. "After the communion the pyx containing the blessed sacrament is left on the table of the altar."[34] Once the prayer after Communion is prayed from the presidential chair, the presider "returns to the altar, genuflects, and incenses the blessed sacrament."[35]

He receives the humeral veil, covers the pyx, and becomes part of a procession from the altar "through the main body of the church to the chapel of reservation."[36] Once in the chapel, the pyx is placed in the tabernacle and incensed, after which the tabernacle doors are closed and a lamp is lit to "burn perpetually before the blessed sacrament."[37] The procession then returns to the church "by the shorter route"[38] for the blessing and dismissal.

There are no words of explanation given and no blessing is pronounced, for "when a church is dedicated or blessed, all the appointments that are already in place are considered to be blessed along with the church."[39] The movement from the altar, where the Eucharistic action has taken place, to the chapel of reservation speaks for itself and clearly distinguishes the active participation of all in the Eucharistic celebration from the participation of all in the adoration of the Eucharist. "The place of reservation is inaugurated by using it."[40]

This rite also emphasizes the fact that Eucharistic reservation flows from Eucharistic celebration. The church building is constructed to facilitate the active participation of all; the chapel for reservation is designed for individual devotion. "Active and static aspects of the same reality cannot claim the same human attention at the same time."[41]

Holy Thursday Model

The rite of "Inauguration of the Blessed Sacrament Chapel" is crafted from the Holy Thursday procession from the altar to the place of reposition. After Communion the Eucharist, a sufficient amount of which should be consecrated at this celebration for Communion of all on Good Friday,[42] is incensed and carried through the church "to the place of reposition prepared in a chapel suitably decorated for the occasion."[43]

Once the chapel is reached, the sacrament is incensed and then placed in the tabernacle. After a period of silent prayer the ministers genuflect and leave.[44]

The priority given to the celebration of the Eucharist is found in one of the rubrics, which states that "the tabernacle should be entirely empty."[45] The procession from the altar to the place of reservation demonstrates that adoration of the Eucharist flows from its celebration. And, finally, that the reservation of the Eucharist is for a purpose: in the case of Holy Thursday, the Eucharist is reserved for Communion on Good Friday, since "according to the Church's ancient tradition, the sacraments are not celebrated"[46] on this day; in the case of the inauguration of a Blessed Sacrament chapel, the Eucharist is reserved primarily for the administration of Viaticum and secondarily for the giving of Communion and the adoration of the Lord Jesus Christ, who is present in the sacrament.[47]

Blessing a New Tabernacle

The rite of "Inauguration of a Blessed Sacrament Chapel" "does not provide . . . for the blessing of a tabernacle but suggests a moment of silent prayer, the sign-gesture that fittingly corresponds to one of the ends of the eucharistic reservation";[48] however, when a new tabernacle is installed, "there is an opportunity to teach the faithful the importance" of this appointment "by means of the celebration of a blessing."[49] The "Order for the Blessing of a New Tabernacle" most fittingly takes place "in conjunction with the celebration of Mass."[50]

After the homily the presider offers a short prayer of blessing, which concludes the general intercessions.

> Lord and Father of all holiness,
> from whom the true bread from heaven has come down to us,
> bless us and the tabernacle we have prepared
> for the sacrament of Christ's body and blood.
> Through our adoration of your Son present in the eucharist,
> lead us to a closer union with the mystery of redemption.[51]

This prayer of blessing emphasizes one of the secondary reasons for reservation of the Eucharist, namely adoration.

After the prayer "the celebrant places incense in the censer and incenses the tabernacle."[52] Nothing else is done until after Communion, when "a pyx or ciborium containing the blessed sacrament is left on the altar table."[53] Like the procession outlined in the rite of "Inauguration of a New Blessed Sacrament Chapel," and like the Holy Thursday procession to the place of reservation, "there may be a procession . . . to the chapel or place where the new tabernacle has been installed."[54]

"When the procession has reached the place where the tabernacle is, the celebrant places the pyx or ciborium in the tabernacle and leaves the door open. After placing incense in the censer, he kneels and incenses the blessed sacrament. After a suitable pause for all to pray in silence, the celebrant closes the tabernacle door."[55] When there is no procession, all is carried out as outlined above after the prayer after Communion. In either case, then the presider or deacon issues the invitation to all present to receive a blessing.

Prayers of Blessing

These suggested prayers of blessing contain a wealth of Eucharistic theology. The first refers to the "Son" who "was the true and living temple on earth." The presider prays that all will be made holy "through Christ's death and resurrection, the mysteries" which are honored when all "adore him."[56] In this prayer the people are referred to as the new temple of Christ's presence, his body, which becomes holy through the paschal mystery.

The second prayer of blessing recalls the ascension of Christ into heaven "before the eyes of his disciples . . . to prepare a place" for all, and the fact that he "is present here, invisible in the sacrament of the altar, to bring . . . the grace that comes from his sacrifice alone," to help and strengthen everyone always.[57] The real presence of the Lord under the form of bread is emphasized by this prayer.

The final prayer of blessing echoes Johannine Eucharistic references to "the inexhaustible fountain of living water, leaping up to provide eternal life." The prayer is for "all who come . . . to consider prayerfully the work of their salvation." The "Lord present in the eucharist," which is nourishing food and drink from the altar, continues to provide "living water, leaping up to provide eternal life" during prayerful adoration.[58]

Prayer over the People

In place of the threefold prayer of blessing, a prayer over the people may be used. This prayer makes reference to the paschal mystery:

Lord,
grant to your servants
a constant deepening in faith and in grace,
so that whenever we honor
your Son's loving presence among us,
we will be led to a more fruitful sharing
in the memorial of our redemption.[59]

After the prayers of blessing or the prayer over the people, all are dismissed in the usual way. It can readily been seen both from the structure of the rite and the words of the prayers that the ceremony of blessing a new tabernacle illustrates how Eucharistic reservation flows from Eucharistic celebration.

Praxis

From this understanding of the theology of Eucharist and the rites of inaugurating a new chapel of reservation and blessing a new tabernacle, there flows a definite practice. As with all the revisions of Vatican Council II, the theological background is given as a reason for the praxis which follows.

Only One Tabernacle

"As a rule, each church should have only one tabernacle."[60] "There should be only one tabernacle in a church building,"[61] just as "it is better to erect one altar only, so that in the one assembly of the people of God the one altar may signify our one Savior Jesus Christ and the one eucharist of the Church."[62] It is the one community of the faithful, who gathers together under the leadership of one shepherd, the bishop, or his representative, the pastor, and celebrates the one Eucharist. Therefore, in order to be faithful to the signs of unity and the purposes of Eucharistic reservation, there should be only one tabernacle in a church complex.

Design

"The tabernacle, as a receptacle for the reservation of the eucharist, should be solid and unbreakable, dignified and properly ornamented."[63] "The eucharist is to be reserved in a single, solid, unbreakable tabernacle."[64] Its size should be determined by its function, namely, to reserve only enough Eucharistic bread for Viaticum, the Communion of the people outside of the Eucharistic celebration, and adoration. On occasion, the Eucharistic wine may be reserved for Communion to the sick "who are unable to receive it under the species of bread." In this case "the Blood of the Lord should be kept in a properly covered chalice and placed in the taberncale after Mass. It should be taken to the sick person only if contained in a vessel which is closed in such a way as to eliminate all danger of spilling."[65]

Placement

The ideal placement of the tabernacle is in "a room or chapel specifically designed and separate from the major space" of the church "so that no confusion can take place between the celebration of the Eucharist and reservation."[66]

"The place . . . where the Blessed Sacrament is reserved in the tabernacle should be truly prominent. It ought to be suitable for private prayer so that the faithful may easily and fruitfully, by private devotion also, continue to honor our Lord in this sacrament. It is therefore recommended that, as far as possible, the tabernacle be placed in a chapel distinct from the middle or central part of the church."[67]

Only when no other chapel is available for Eucharistic reservation "because of the structure of the church"[68] is the tabernacle to be placed in the main body of the church. In this case, "the sacrament should be reserved at an altar or elsewhere, in keeping with local custom, and in a part of the church that is worthy and properly adorned."[69]

The first choice for the placement of the tabernacle in a church which has no specific chapel or room for reservation is somewhere other than the altar where the Eucharist is celebrated. In older churches a side altar can serve this purpose. The second choice is near the altar where the Eucharist is celebrated; however, this choice should be made as a last resort in order to avoid the confusion that can take place between the celebration of the Eucharist and the reservation of the Eucharist.

"Having the Eucharist reserved in a place apart does not mean it has been relegated to a secondary place of no importance. Rather, a space carefully designed and appointed can give proper attention to the reserved sacrament."[70]

The tabernacle should be placed on an altar only in an exceptional case, because "the altar is a place for action" and "not for reservation."[71]

> In the celebration of Mass the principal modes of worship by which Christ is present to his church are gradually revealed. First of all, Christ is seen to be present among the faithful gathered in his name; then in his Word, as

the Scriptures are read and explained; in the person of the minister; finally and in a unique way under the species of the Eucharist. Consequently, by reason of the symbolism, it is more in keeping with the nature of the celebration that the eucharistic presence of Christ, which is the fruit of the consecration and should be seen as such, should not be on the altar from the very beginning of Mass through the reservation of the sacred species in the tabernacle.[72]

The best placement of the tabernacle, therefore, would seem to be "in a wall niche, on a pillar, eucharistic tower."[73] "If iconography or statuary are present, they should not obscure the primary focus of reservation."[74]

Signs of Eucharistic Reservation

"According to traditional usage, an oil lamp or lamp with a wax candle is to burn constantly near the tabernacle as a sign of the honor which is shown to the Lord."[75] This light must consist of either a real oil lamp or real candles. It may not consist of an electric sanctuary lamp.[76] Otherwise the demands of quality and appropriateness, explained by *Environment and Art in Catholic Worship,* are violated.[77] "The quality and appropriateness demanded by the Church's liturgy rule out anything fake, shoddy, pretentious, or lacking in a kind of artistic 'transparency.' "[78]

A tabernacle veil can also be used to indicate the presence of the Eucharist in the tabernacle.[79] The use of a veil would be determined by the size and placement of the tabernacle as well as by its artistic design.

Access

Because the Eucharist is reserved for adoration by the faithful, "pastors should see to it that all churches . . . remain open for at least several hours in the morning and evening so that it may be easy for the faithful to pray before the Blessed Sacrament."[80] The chapel or room for reservation "should offer easy access from the porch areas, garden or street as well as the main space. The devotional character of the space should create an atmosphere of warmth while acknowledging the mystery of the Lord. It should support private meditation without distractions."[81]

Other Considerations

The Eucharist is not reserved from one celebration to another in order to facilitate the Communion of the people. The documents of the Church make no provision for trips to the tabernacle during the Eucharistic celebration before the Communion of the faithful. "The more perfect form of participation in the Mass" takes place when the "faithful, after the priest's communion, receive the Lord's Body from the same sacrifice."[82] Therefore, "care should be taken to enable the faithful to communicate with hosts consecrated during the Mass."[83] Furthermore, "recently baked bread . . . should ordinarily be consecrated in every eucharistic celebration."[84]

"Holy communion has a more complete form as a sign when it is received under both kinds. For in this manner of reception a fuller light shines on the sign of the eucharistic banquet. Moreover there is a clearer expression of that will by which the new and everlasting covenant is ratified in the blood of the Lord and of the relationship of the eucharistic banquet to the eschatological banquet in the Father's kingdom."[85]

Thus, through the signs of sharing both the bread and the chalice "communion will stand out more clearly as a sharing in the sacrifice actually being celebrated."[86]

There is no mention in the General Instruction of the Roman Missal of a trip to the tabernacle by the presider after Communion. However, *This Holy and Living Sacrifice: Directory for the Celebration and Reception of Communion Under Both Kinds,* states, "After Communion the eucharistic bread that remains is to be stored in the tabernacle."[87] Particles that remain are gathered and either consumed or taken by a minister to the place where the Eucharist is reserved.

In most cases it would seem that the particles are to be consumed. Only when Communion is to be taken as Viaticum to the sick, for Communion of the people when Mass cannot be celebrated, or for adoration should a trip be made to the tabernacle. Otherwise, the reasons for Eucharistic reservation are violated. The procession to the tabernacle is best done by a Eucharistic minister or a minister other than the presider.

"When there remains more consecrated wine than was necessary, the ministers shall consume it immediately at a side table before the Prayer After Communion, while the vessels themselves may be purified after Mass."[88] Even when there are no Eucharistic ministers, it is preferable that the vessels be "purified by the priest or else by the deacon or acolyte after the communion or after Mass, if possible at a side table."[89]

Conclusion

The reverence shown to the reserved Eucharist in the tabernacle flows from the theology of Eucharist and the theology of the tabernacle as found in the documents of the Church. The theology of Eucharist and the theology of the tabernacle should inform praxis. Active participation in the Eucharist leads to its reservation.

Notes

1. GIRM, no. 276.
2. HCWEM, no. 9.
3. IWEM, no. 49.
4. Ibid., no. 50.
5. EACW, no. 78.
6. Ibid.
7. Ibid.
8. Ibid., no. 79.
9. BB, no. 1192.
10. DCA, "Dedication of a Church," ch. 2, no. 79.
11. Ibid., no. 19; cf. no. 2.
12. HCWEM, no. 2.
13. IWEM, no. 6.
14. EACW, no. 78.
15. DCA:C, 35.
16. EACW, no. 78.
17. DCA:C, 35.
18. IWEM, no. 49.
19. HCWEM, no. 6.
20. TS, Easter Triduum, Evening Mass of the Lord's Supper.
21. HCWEM, no. 2.
22. Ibid., no. 94.
23. Ibid., no. 83.
24. Ibid., no. 82.
25. GIRM, no. 283.
26. IWEM, no. 31.
27. Ibid., no. 3.
28. Ibid., no. 8.
29. IWEM, no. 11.
30. HCWEM, no. 9.
31. EACW, no. 78.
32. DCA, "Dedication of a Church," ch. 2, no. 3.
33. DCA:C, 35.
34. DCA, "Dedication of a Church," ch. 2, no. 79.
35. Ibid., no. 80.
36. Ibid.
37. Ibid., no. 81.
38. Ibid., no. 82.
39. BB, no. 1150.

40. DCA:C, 35.

41. EACW, no. 78.

42. TS, Easter Triduum, Evening Mass of the Lord's Supper.

43. Ibid.

44. Cf. TS, Easter Triduum, Evening Mass of the Lord's Supper.

45. TS, Easter Triduum, Evening Mass of the Lord's Supper.

46. TS, Good Friday, Celebration of the Lord's Passion, no. 1.

47. Cf. HCWEM, no. 5.

48. DCA:C, 35.

49. BB, no. 1150.

50. Ibid., no. 1193.

51. Ibid., no. 1194.

52. Ibid., no. 1195.

53. Ibid., no. 1196.

54. Ibid.

55. Ibid., no. 1197.

56. Ibid., no. 1198.

57. Ibid.

58. Ibid.

59. Ibid., no. 1199.

60. IWEM, no. 52; cf. GIRM, no. 277; cf. HCWEM, no. 10; cf. CCL, 938:1.

61. EACW, no. 80.

62. DCA, "Dedication of an Altar," ch. 4, no. 7.

63. EACW, no. 80; cf. CCL, 938:3.

64. GIRM, no. 277; cf. CCL, 938:3.

65. IWEM, no. 41; cf. THLS, no. 37.

66. EACW, no. 78.

67. IWEM, no. 53; cf. CCL, 938:2.

68. GIRM, no. 276.

69. Ibid.

70. EACW, no. 78.

71. Ibid., no. 80.

72. IWEM, no. 55.

73. EACW, no. 80.

74. Ibid., no. 79.

75. HCWEM, no. 11; cf. IWEM, no. 57; cf. EACW, no. 80.

76. Cf. BCLN 18 (December 1982) 47–48.

77. Cf. EACW, nos. 19–26.

78. BCLN 18 (December 1982) 48.

79. Cf. IWEM, no. 57; HCWEM, no. 11.

80. IWEM, no. 51.

81. EACW, no. 79.

82. CSL, no. 55.

83. IWEM, no. 31; cf. GIRM, no. 56h.

84. HCWEM, no. 13.

85. GIRM, no. 240.
86. Ibid., no. 56h.
87. THLS, no. 36.
88. Ibid.
89. GIRM, no. 238; cf. GIRM, no. 120.

Chapter 7

Christ the Light

Ecclesial Documents

The norm of active participation by everyone in the liturgy is particularly emphasized in Chapter 5 of The Constitution on the Sacred Liturgy, "The Liturgical Year." "Once each week, on the day which [Holy Mother Church] has called the Lord's Day, she keeps the memory of the Lord's resurrection. She also celebrates it once every year, together with his blessed passion, at Easter, that most solemn of all feasts. . . . Recalling the mysteries of the redemption, she opens up to the faithful the riches of her Lord's powers and merits, so that these are in some way made present for all time; the faithful lay hold of them and are filled with saving grace."[1]

"The Church celebrates the paschal mystery every seventh day, which day is appropriately called the Lord's Day or Sunday. For on this day Christ's faithful are bound to come together into one place. They should listen to the word of God and take part in the Eucharist, thus calling to mind the passion, resurrection, and glory of the Lord Jesus, and giving thanks to God who 'has begotten them again, through the resurrection of Christ from the dead, unto a living hope' (1 Pet 1:3)."[2]

The norm of active participation is further fleshed out in three documents: (1) the General Instruction of the Roman Missal, (2) *Environment and Art in Catholic Worship,* and (3) "Preparing and Celebrating the Paschal Feasts."

"Preparing and Celebrating the Paschal Feasts" repeatedly encourages the active participation of the people. This is particularly encouraged for the Easter Vigil: "The Easter Vigil liturgy should be celebrated in such a

way as to offer to the Christian people the riches of the prayers and rites. It is therefore important that authenticity be respected, that the participation of the faithful be promoted and that the celebration should not take place without servers, readers and choir exercising their role."[3]

Furthermore, "it would be desirable if on occasion provision were made for several communities to assemble in one church wherever their proximity one to another or small numbers mean that a full and festive celebration could not otherwise take place. Pastors should be advised that in giving catechesis to the people they should be taught to participate in the vigil in its entirety."[4]

Our consideration here is the theology of the Easter candle found in the documents of the Church and the praxis which should flow from this theology. After exploring the theology of the Easter candle as presented in the documents following Vatican Council II, the praxis, which either fosters or impedes active participation, will be examined.

Theology of the Easter Candle

Every ritual can be subdivided into sign and symbol. A sign is a thing, object, person, or circumstance that represents or points toward another thing, object, person, or circumstance. In contrast, a symbol is an action that reveals a relationship; it is not a thing. For example, the Easter candle is a sign of Christ risen from the dead, but the symbol is the proclamation in song that Christ is our light and the sharing of the light (by lighting the individual candles) of all present for the Easter Vigil.

Environment and Art in Catholic Worship states that "every word, gesture, movement, object, appointment must be real in the sense that it is our own. It must come from the deepest understanding of ourselves."[5] This "deepest understanding of ourselves" is reflected in the Easter candle, its preparation, its placement in the church, its use, and its candlestand.

Prepared Once a Year

According to "Preparing and Celebrating the Paschal Feasts," "The paschal candle should be prepared, which for effective symbolism must be made of wax, never be artificial, be renewed each year, be only one in number and be of sufficiently large size so that it may evoke the truth that Christ is the light of the world. It is blessed with the signs and words prescribed in the missal."[6]

The Easter candle is prepared and blessed only once a year, during the Easter Vigil,

> on this most holy night,
> when our Lord Jesus Christ passed from death to life,
> . . . the passover of the Lord.[7]

The preparation of the Easter candle is part of the service of light, which begins with the preparation of "a large fire . . . in a suitable place outside the church."[8] The flames of this new fire "should be such that they genuinely dispel the darkness and light up the night,"[9] for they represent "the light of the glory" of the Father; the Son, who is "the light of the world"; the desire that they "inflame . . . with new hope" those present; the wish they they "purify [the] minds" of the congregation; and the desire of all to be brought "one day to the feast of eternal light."[10]

Once the new fire has been kindled and blessed, the Easter candle, the means of getting the new fire and all it represents from outside the darkened church to inside the church where it will illuminate the whole church and "dispel the darkness of . . . hearts and minds,"[11] is prepared.

Signs Traced on the Candle

In order "to stress the dignity and significance of the Easter candle" the presider may use a number of "symbolic rites."[12] He "cuts a cross in the wax with a stylus" and "then . . . traces the Greek letter alpha above the cross, the letter omega below, and the numerals of the current year between the arms of the cross."[13]

While tracing the vertical arm of the cross the presider says, "Christ yesterday and today"; while cutting the horizontal arm, "the beginning and the end"; while writing "alpha" above the cross, "Alpha"; and while writing "omega" below the cross, "and Omega"; while displaying the first numeral of the current year in the upper left corner of the cross, "all time belongs to him"; while recording the second numeral of the current year in the upper right corner of the cross, "and all the ages"; while cutting the third numeral into the lower left corner of the cross, "to him be glory and power"; and while placing the last numeral in the lower right corner of the cross, "through every age for ever. Amen."[14]

The phrases used while tracing the cross, the alpha and the omega, and the current year on the Easter candle are expansions and combinations of verses found in the Book of Revelation and the Book of the Prophet Isaiah. " 'I am the Alpha and the Omega,' says the Lord God, 'the one who is and who was and who is to come, the almighty' " (Rev 1:8) is also found in Revelation 1:17 and 21:6. "I am the Alpha and the Omega, the first and the last, the beginning and the end" (Rev 22:13) is echoed earlier in Revelation 2:8 and in Isaiah 41:4, 44:6, and 48:12.

"When the cross and other marks have been made, the priest may insert five grains of incense in the candle . . . in the form of a cross."[15] He inserts the first grain at the top of the vertical arm of the cross saying, "By his holy"; the second where the horizontal and vertical arms meet, "and glorious wounds"; the third at the bottom of the vertical arm of the cross, "may Christ our Lord"; the fourth at the left of the horizontal arm, "guard us"; and the last at the right of the horizontal arm, "and keep us. Amen."[16] The candle is then lighted from the new fire.[17]

By tracing the cross on the Easter candle, "the light of Christ, rising in glory,"[18] and inserting the five grains of incense in the place of the wounds of Christ (head, side, hands, and feet), the Church declares that the One who was crucified is now risen from the dead. The paschal candle, therefore, represents "the passover of the Lord"[19] from death to life; it gives honor to "the memory of his death and resurrection";[20] and represents the hope that all people will "share his victory over death and live with him for ever in God."[21]

Furthermore, the paschal mystery signified by the paschal candle will be celebrated in the baptism of the elect, who "through baptism and confirmation . . . are inserted into the paschal mystery of Christ, dying, buried and raised with him,"[22] after which, later in the Easter Vigil, each will receive a candle lighted from the Easter candle. It will also be remembered by the assembly as they are reminded that

> through the paschal mystery [they] have been buried with Christ in baptism, so that [they] may rise with him to a new life"[23]

while all hold "lighted candles and renew their baptismal profession of faith"[24] and are sprinkled with the water that has given them "a new birth by water and the Holy Spirit."[25]

The incense grains are used on the paschal candle to mark the five wounds of the crucified Christ. "Fire recalls the Holy Spirit, that fire sent upon the Church by Christ, risen and seated at his Father's right hand (see Acts 2:1-3). The fragrance acceptable to the Father is that which comes from Christ's Easter sacrifice, as we read in St. Paul: 'Follow the way of love, even as Christ loved you. He gave himself for us an offering to God, a gift of pleasing fragrance' (Eph 5:2)."[26]

Furthermore, "the Book of Revelation (5:8; 8:3-4) says that incense—besides symbolizing the 'acceptable fragrance'—is also a symbol of prayer that rises to God."[27] After the paschal candle leads the procession of the people into the church, it may be incensed.[28] "Just as the children of Israel were guided at night by a pillar of fire, so similarly Christians follow the risen Christ."[29]

Three times the candle is declared to be "Christ our light,"[30] after which "the light from the paschal candle should be gradually passed to the candles which it is fitting that all present should hold in their hands."[31] "Christ the Light is symbolized in and praised by means of the paschal candle. Only the light of his resurrection illumines the darkness of the night and enlightens the assembled Church."[32]

For this reason, "the entire celebration of the Easter Vigil takes place at night. It should not begin before nightfall; it should end before daybreak on Sunday."[33] "To celebrate the Easter Vigil before nightfall or to conclude it with the light of dawn at a 'sunrise service' misses the mark" of the symbolism of the paschal candle.[34]

"The Passover vigil, in which the Hebrews kept watch for the Lord's Passover, which was to free them from slavery to pharaoh, is an annual commemoration. It prefigured the true Pasch of Christ that was to come, the night that is of true liberation, in which 'destroying the bond of death, Christ rose as victor from the depths.' "[35] "The full meaning of the vigil is a waiting for the coming of the Lord";[36] it is a commemoration of that "holy night when the Lord rose from the dead [and] . . . the church keeps vigil, waiting for the resurrection of the Lord, and celebrates the sacraments of Christian initiation."[37]

The Easter Proclamation

Once the new fire has been kindled, the Easter candle has been prepared, and the assembly has entered the darkened church proclaiming Christ, represented by the paschal candle, to be the light, "the deacon makes the Easter proclamation, which tells by means of a great poetic text the whole Easter mystery placed in the context of the economy of salvation."[38] This text is divided into two parts.

The first part is the official proclamation of the resurrection: "Jesus Christ, our King, is risen!"[39] The "heavenly powers" are exhorted to "rejoice," and the "choirs of angels" are exhorted to "sing." Likewise, the "earth in shining splendor" rejoices, because it is "radiant in the brightness of [the] King" and its "darkness vanishes for ever." "Mother Church" rejoices too, because "the risen Savior shines upon [her]." Finally, the assembly is exhorted to "resound with joy" and to echo "the mighty song of all God's people."[40]

After the deacon's invitation to the congregation "standing . . . in [the] holy light" (of the Easter candle) to ask "God for mercy, that he may give his unworthy minister grace to sing his Easter praises,"[41] the second part of the Easter proclamation begins.

This part of the Easter proclamation is euchological, that is, it begins with a preface-type dialogue and introduction and is followed by the thanksgiving, the anamnesis, the institution narrative, the offering, an intercession, and the doxology.

DIALOGUE, INTRODUCTION, AND THANKSGIVING

The initial dialogue of this part of the Easter proclamation is identical to that which begins every Eucharistic Prayer. The "it is truly right that with full hearts and minds and voices we should praise the unseen God, the all-powerful Father, and his only Son, our Lord Jesus Christ"[42] echoes the "Father, all-powerful and ever-living God, we do well always and everywhere to give you thanks" (sometimes to which is added "through Jesus Christ our Lord" or another similar phrase), which introduces every preface[43] and which "praises the Father and gives thanks to him for the whole work of salvation or for some special aspect of it."[44]

The element of thanksgiving continues in praise of "Christ [who] has ransomed us with his blood, and paid for us the price of Adam's sin." Likewise, the "wonderful . . . care" of the Father and "his boundless . . . merciful love" prompted him "to ransom a slave" by giving away his Son.[45]

ANAMNESIS

In the anamnesis "the Church keeps [Christ's] memorial by recalling especially his passion, resurrection, and ascension."[46] The deacon proclaims,

> This is our passover feast,
> when Christ, the true Lamb, is slain,
> whose blood consecrates the homes of all believers.

> This is the night when first you saved our fathers:
> you freed the people of Israel from their slavery
> and led them dry-shod through the sea. . . .

> This is the night when Jesus Christ
> broke the chains of death
> and rose triumphant from the grave.[47]

INSTITUTION NARRATIVE

The institution narrative in this song is not unlike that found in the Eucharistic Prayers, which recall the institution of the Eucharist by Christ on the night before he died. This institution narrative establishes and recalls the first Easter Vigil as "Christ, [the] Morning Star . . . came back from the dead and shed his peaceful light on all. . . ."[48] This is accomplished through the repetition of "this is the night" and the making present of the Old Testament events of Passover and the Exodus, which was guided by "the pillar of fire"[49] and is now guided by the light of the Easter candle.

The Passover and Exodus are made present on this "night truly blessed when heaven is wedded to earth and man [and woman] is [are] reconciled with God" in "Christians everywhere," who, "washed clean of sin and freed from all defilement, is [are] restored to grace and grow together in holiness."[50] Through the waters of baptism on this "most blessed of all nights, chosen by God to see Christ rising from the dead,"[51] evil is dispelled, guilt is washed away, lost innocence is restored, mourners are brought joy, hatred is cast out, peace is brought to all, and earthly pride is humbled.[52]

In fact, this night is so filled with power over sin and death that the deacon can proclaim:

> O happy fault, O necessary sin of Adam,
> which gained for us so great a Redeemer![53]

OFFERING

In this prayer "the Church—and in particular the Church here and now assembled—offers the spotless victim to the Father in the Holy Spirit. The Church's intention is that the faithful not only offer this victim but also learn to offer themselves and so to surrender themselves, through Christ the mediator, to an ever more complete union with the Father and with each other, so that at last God may be all in all."[54]

"In the joy of this night," the "heavenly Father" is asked to "receive [the] evening sacrifice of praise, . . . [the] Church's solemn offering," the "Easter candle, a flame divided but undimmed, a pillar of fire that glows to the honor of God."[55]

INTERCESSION

The Father is asked to "let it mingle with the lights of heaven and continue bravely burning to dispel the darkness of this night," so that "the Morning Star which never sets" will "find this flame still burning."[56]

DOXOLOGY

In the last part of the Easter proclamation, the Father is praised and Christ is declared to be "that Morning Star, who came back from the dead, and shed his peaceful light on all," the Son of God, "who lives and reigns for ever and ever. Amen."[57]

The "amen" of this prayer of blessing of the Easter candle, like the "amen" which concludes Eucharistic Prayers, concludes the service of light. Therefore, it can be readily seen that this first part of the Easter Vigil, which "consists of symbolic acts and gestures," requires "that they be performed in all their fullness and nobility so that their meaning, as explained by the introductory words of the celebrant and the liturgical prayers, may be truly understood by the faithful.''[58]

Lowering the Candle into the Water

During the blessing of water of the liturgy of baptism, the third part of the Easter Vigil, the presider ''may lower the Easter candle into the water either once or three times,'' as he prays, ''We ask you, Father, with your Son to send the Holy Spirit upon the waters of this font.'' Then, while holding the candle in the water, he says, ''May all who are buried with Christ in the death of baptism rise also with him to newness of life.''[59]

This ritual action is done to indicate that through Christ's death and resurrection the water is made fertile for those who will be baptized, ''inserted into the paschal mystery of Christ, dying, buried and raised with him.''[60] ''Christ's passover and ours is . . . celebrated . . . when the Christian initiation of adults is held or at least the baptism of infants.''[61]

Praxis

From this understanding of the theology of the Easter candle, there flows a definite practice. As with all the revisions inaugurated by Vatican Council II, the theological background is given as a reason for the praxis which follows.

Made of Wax

The Easter candle ''must be made of wax'' and must ''never be artificial.''[62] ''Candles made of wax are to be used in the celebration of the Mass and other liturgical rites. . . . Because of their very nature, imitations of candles should not be used in the liturgy as, for example, 'permanent' paschal candles.''[63]

Authentic liturgy demands quality and appropriateness. ''Quality means love and care in the making of something, honesty and genuineness with any materials used, and the artist's special gift in producing a harmonious whole, a well-crafted work.''[64] Appropriateness indicates that a work of art ''must be capable of bearing the weight of mystery, awe, reverence, and wonder which the liturgical action expresses,'' and ''it must clearly *serve* ritual action which has its own structure, rhythm and movement.''[65]

Quality, therefore, ''rules out anything trivial and self-centered, anything fake, cheap or shoddy, anything pretentious or superficial.''[66] Appropriateness "refers both to the physical environment of public worship and to any art forms which might be employed as part of the liturgical action."[67] It is impossible to "stress the dignity and significance of the Easter candle"[68] when it is an imitation or artificial.

Likewise, in order for its symbolism to be effective, it must "be renewed each year, be only one in number and be of sufficiently large size so that it may evoke the truth that Christ is the light of the world."[69] This means that the Easter candle used throughout the Easter season and the rest of the year is to be prepared and blessed "with the signs and words prescribed in the missal."[70]

There should be only one Easter candle in a church building even if the baptistery is located in a separate part of the church complex. Old Easter candles should be appropriately and reverently discarded.

The candle must be large if it is to be recognized as sacred by the community. The Easter candle must evoke the Exodus "pillar of fire," after which it is modeled. "Just as the children of Israel were guided at night by a pillar of fire, so similarly Christians follow the risen Christ."[71] Whatever its style or type, no paschal candle "has a right to a place in liturgical celebration if it is not of high quality and if it is not appropriate,"[72] that is, if it does not by itself sing "Christ our light."[73] It "should be not only suitable for its purpose but also capable of making a visual or other sensory contribution to the beauty of the action."[74]

Location

"The paschal candle has its proper place either by the ambo or by the altar."[75] During the Easter Vigil, the deacon may place it "on a stand in the middle of the sanctuary or near the lectern."[76] "The Easter Candle and its standard call for very special dimensions and design. They occupy a central location in the assembly during the Easter season"[77] and "should be lit at least in all the more solemn liturgical celebrations of the season until Pentecost Sunday, whether at Mass or at morning and evening prayer."[78]

It is also important to note that the pre–Vatican II practice of extinguishing the paschal candle after the proclamation of the gospel on Ascension Thursday has been abrogated.

After Evening Prayer II of Pentecost Sunday, "the end of the Easter season, the Easter candle should be kept in the baptistery with due honor"[79] "in such a way that it can be lighted for the celebration of baptism and so that from it the candles for the newly baptized can easily be lighted."[80]

Use for Funerals

"In the celebration of funerals the paschal candle should be placed near the coffin."[81] "The Easter candle reminds the faithful of Christ's undying presence among them, of his victory over sin and death, and of their share in that victory by virtue of their initiation. It recalls the Easter Vigil, the night when the Church awaits the Lord's resurrection and when new light for the living and the dead is kindled. During the funeral liturgy and also during the Vigil service, when celebrated in the church, the Easter candle may be placed beforehand near the position the coffin will occupy at the conclusion of the procession."[82] The paschal candle indicates "that the death of a Christian is his [or her] own passover."[83]

"The paschal candle should not otherwise be lit nor placed in the sanctuary outside the Easter season."[84]

Conclusion

The reverence shown to the Easter candle flows from the theology of the paschal candle, which is found in the documents of the Church. The theology of the Easter candle should inform praxis, which includes the annual preparation and blessing of the candle, its use during the Easter Vigil and the Easter season, and its use for baptisms and funerals. The Christian participates in worship around the assembly's common light, "the radiance of the risen Christ,"[85] which is "a flame divided but undimmed, a pillar of fire that glows to the honor of God."[86]

Notes

1. CSL, no. 102.
2. Ibid., no. 106.
3. PCPF, no. 93.
4. Ibid., nos. 94 and 95.
5. EACW, no. 14.
6. PCPF, no. 82.
7. TS, The Easter Vigil, no. 8.
8. Ibid., no. 7.
9. PCPF, no. 82.
10. TS, The Easter Vigil, no. 8.
11. Ibid., no. 12.
12. Ibid., no. 10.
13. Ibid.

14. Ibid.
15. Ibid., no. 11.
16. Ibid.
17. Cf. TS, The Easter Vigil, nos. 9 and 12.
18. TS, The Easter Vigil, no. 12.
19. Ibid., no. 8.
20. Ibid.
21. Ibid.
22. PCPF, no. 80.
23. TS, The Easter Vigil, cf. no. 46.
24. Ibid.
25. Ibid.
26. DCA:C, 29.
27. Ibid.
28. Cf. TS, The Easter Vigil, no. 17.
29. PCPF, no. 83.
30. TS, The Easter Vigil, nos. 14 and 15.
31. PCPF, no. 83.
32. BCLN 22 (February 1986) 8.
33. PCPF, no. 78.
34. BCLN 22 (February 1986) 8.
35. PCPF, no. 79.
36. Ibid., no. 80.
37. Ibid., no. 77.
38. Ibid., no. 84.
39. TS, The Easter Vigil, no. 18.
40. Ibid.
41. Ibid.
42. Ibid.
43. TS, Preface for Advent I, ff.
44. GIRM, no. 55a.
45. TS, The Easter Vigil, no. 18.
46. GIRM, no. 55e.
47. TS, The Easter Vigil, no. 18.
48. Ibid.
49. Ibid.
50. Ibid.
51. Ibid.
52. Cf. TS, The Easter Vigil, no. 18.
53. TS, The Easter Vigil, no. 18.
54. GIRM, no. 55f.
55. TS, The Easter Vigil, no. 18.
56. Ibid.
57. Ibid.
58. PCPF, no. 82.

59. TS, The Easter Vigil, no. 42.
60. PCPF, no. 80.
61. Ibid., no. 88.
62. Ibid., no. 82.
63. BCLN 20 (November 1984) 44.
64. EACW, no. 20.
65. Ibid., no. 21.
66. Ibid., no. 22.
67. Ibid., no. 23.
68. TS, The Easter Vigil, no. 10.
69. PCPF, no. 82.
70. Ibid.
71. Ibid., no. 83.
72. EACW, no. 19.
73. TS, The Easter Vigil, nos. 14 and 15.
74. EACW, no. 84.
75. PCPF, no. 99.
76. TS, The Easter Vigil, no. 16.
77. EACW, no. 90.
78. PCPF, no. 99.
79. TS, Pentecost, Mass During the Day.
80. CIGI, no. 25; cf. PCPF, no. 99; cf. RCIA, no. 230; cf RBC, no. 64.
81. PCPF, no. 99; cf. TS, Pentecost, Mass During the Day.
82. OCF, no. 35.
83. PCPF, no. 99.
84. Ibid.
85. TS, The Easter Vigil, no. 32.
86. Ibid., no. 18.

Chapter 8

Clothing the Assembly

Ecclesial Documents

The norm of active participation pertaining to vesture is fleshed out in various documents of Vatican II, particularly in two: (1) the General Instruction of the Roman Missal and (2) *Environment and Art in Catholic Worship*.

Vatican II Documents

The Constitution on the Sacred Liturgy makes clear that "the liturgy . . . is rightly seen as an exercise of the priestly office of Jesus Christ. . . . Every liturgical celebration, because it is an action of Christ the Priest and of his Body, which is the Church, is a sacred action surpassing all others. No other action of the Church can equal its efficacy by the same title and to the same degree."[1]

The Decree on the Ministry and Life of Priests emphasizes that "all the faithful are made a holy and kingly priesthood, [and] they offer spiritual sacrifices to God through Jesus Christ. . . . Therefore, there is no such thing as a member that has not a share in the mission of the whole Body. However, the Lord also appointed certain men as ministers, in order that they might be united in one body in which 'all the members have not the same function' (Rom 12:4)."[2]

The liturgy, then, is "an action of the entire people of God, hierarchically organized and acting hierarchically."[3] "Though they differ essentially and not only in degree, the common priesthood of the faithful and the

141

ministerial or hierarchical priesthood are none the less ordered one to another; each in its own proper way shares in the one priesthood of Christ."[4] "Each in his [or her] own way, though not of course indiscriminately, has his [or her] own part to play in the liturgical action. Then, strengthened by the body of Christ in the eucharistic communion, they manifest in a concrete way that unity of the People of God which this holy sacrament aptly signifies and admirably realizes."[5]

The Instruction on the Worship of the Eucharistic Mystery states, "The more clearly the faithful understand the place they occupy in the liturgical community and the part they have to play in the eucharistic action, the more conscious and fruitful will be the active participation which is proper to that community."[6]

Post–Vatican II Documents

The General Instruction of the Roman Missal introduces all of its guidelines with the call for active participation:

> The celebration of Mass, the action of Christ and the people of God arrayed hierarchically, is for the universal and the local Church as well as for each person the center of the whole Christian life. Therefore, it is of the greatest importance that the celebration of the Mass, the Lord's Supper, be so arranged that the ministers and the faithful who take their own proper part in it may more fully receive its good effects. This purpose will best be accomplished if . . . the celebration is planned in such a way that it brings about in the faithful a participation in body and spirit that is conscious, active, full, and motivated by faith, hope, and charity.[7]

This document declares, "The Church desires this kind of participation, the nature of the celebration demands it, and for the Christian people it is a right and duty they have by reason of their baptism. The presence and active participation of the people bring out more plainly the ecclesial nature of the celebration."[8] Active participation must be fostered because "the most powerful experience of the sacred is found in the celebration and the persons celebrating, that is, it is found in the action of the assembly: the living words, the living gestures, the living sacrifice, the living meal."[9]

Our consideration here is the theology of vesture (vestments, banners, hangings, coverings) found in the documents and the praxis which should flow from this theology. Therefore, after exploring the theology of vesture as presented by Vatican Council II, the praxis, which either fosters or impedes active participation, will be examined.

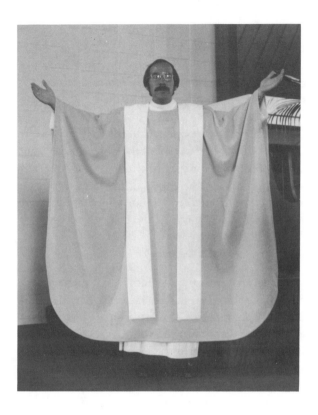

Theology of Vesture

Vestments "symbolize the function proper to each ministry"[10] in the Church. "In the Church, the Body of Christ, not all members have the same function. This diversity of ministries is shown outwardly in worship by the diversity of vestments."[11]

Vesture is also a symbol of service offered by the leader of ritual action.[12] The one who presides has to be "attentive to and present to the entire congregation, the other ministers, and each part of the liturgical action."[13] As the leader, the presider conducts "the various ministers in their specific activity and roles of leadership, as well as the congregation in its common prayer."[14] Therefore, this "service is a function which demands attention from the assembly and which operates in the focal area of the assembly's liturgical action."[15]

The vesture worn by the various ministers is a "helpful aesthetic component of the rite."[16] It "should be not only suitable for its purpose but also capable of making a visual or other sensory contribution to the beauty of the action,"[17] that is, "to the beauty of the rite."[18]

Furthermore, "the color and form of the vestments and their difference from everyday clothing invite an appropriate attention"[19] from the assembly. The attention given those clothed in vestments enables them to better fulfill their roles of leadership.

Vesture is "part of the ritual experience essential to the festive character of a liturgical celebration."[20] "Variety in the color of the vestments is meant to give effective, outward expression to the specific character of the mysteries of the faith being celebrated and, in the course of the year, to a sense of progress in the Christian life."[21] Therefore, "on solemn occasions more precious vestments may be used, even if not of the color of the day."[22]

White Garment

Because all men and women are "incorporated into the Church by Baptism," they "are appointed by their baptismal character to Christian religious worship. . . . By the sacrament of Confirmation they are more perfectly bound to the Church and are endowed with the special strength of the Holy Spirit. Taking part in the eucharistic sacrifice, the source and summit of the Christian life, they offer the divine victim to God and themselves along with it."[23] They exercise this "priesthood, too, by the reception of the sacraments, prayer and thanksgiving, the witness of a holy life, abnegation and active charity."[24]

The faithful, therefore, possess "a royal priesthood to which [they] are consecrated by rebirth and the anointing of the Holy Spirit."[25]"The ministerial priesthood which differs from the common priesthood of the faithful in essence and not merely in degree"[26] presupposes the sacraments of initiation.[27]

For this reason, "the vestment common to ministers of every rank is the alb."[28] The alb is the white garment received in baptism. It is a sign of becoming a new creation and being clothed in Christ. Every time a person in the ministerial priesthood functions, he does so clothed in his baptismal garment. The alb reminds the ministerial priest that he is chosen from the common priesthood of the baptized to serve the baptized.

Praxis

From this understanding of the theology of vesture, there flows a definite practice. As with all the revisions inaugurated by Vatican Council II, the theological background is given as a reason for the praxis which follows.

Symbolic Value

Because vesture is an effective symbol of diversity in ministries, leadership, and function, every vestment "must be real in the sense that it is our own. It must come from the deepest understanding of ourselves (not careless, phony, counterfeit, pretentious, exaggerated, etc.).''[29] In order to practice the theological renewal as defined by the Second Vatican Council, "the opening up of . . . symbols"[30] must take place so that they can be experienced as authentic and so that their symbolic value can be appreciated.[31] The concern must be for "noble simplicity.''[32]

In the case of vesture as in the case of many other symbols, "there is a cultural tendency to minimize.''[33] As explained in *Environment and Art in Catholic Worship,* this leads to two problems.

First, there "is the tendency to duplicate signs and objects, a practice which seems to have multiplied in proportion to the symbols' diminution. (The converse is also true: the multiplication of symbols causes their very diminution.) A symbol claims human attention and consciousness with a power that seems to be adversely affected by overdose.''[34]

Second, there "is a tendency to 'make up' for weak primary symbols by [creating] secondary ones. . . . Peripheral elements frequently get more attention. . . . It is important to focus on central symbols and to allow them to be expressed with the full depth of their vision.''[35]

In order to alleviate these two problems, it is best that vestments "fulfill their function by their color, design and enveloping form,''[36] Indeed, "the beauty of a vestment should derive from its material and design rather than from lavish ornamentation.''[37] In fact, "ornamentation on objects may lessen rather than increase attention to that symbol.''[38]

If this is understood, then there will be no need for "signs, slogans and [secondary] symbols which an unkind history has fastened on [vestments]. The tendency to place symbols upon symbols seems to accompany the symbolic deterioration and diminution"[39] which was explained above.

Priests

The proper vestments for priests are the chasuble and stole and the cope and stole. "The chasuble, worn over the alb and stole ('the priest wears the stole around his neck and hanging down in front'[40]), is the vestment proper to the priest celebrant at Mass and other rites immediately connected with Mass."[41] "The cope is worn by the priest in processions and other services."[42]

Concelebratants

When many priests concelebrate, "the concelebrants may omit the chasuble and simply wear the stole over the alb; but the principal celebrant always wears the chasuble."[43]

In 1977 the Congregation for the Sacraments and Divine Worship approved the use of the chasuble-alb in the dioceses of the United States. The chasuble-alb was permitted to be used "in concelebrations, in Masses for special groups, in celebrations outside a sacred place, and in similar cases where by reason of the place or persons its use seems advisable. Concerning the color of the vestment, it is only required that the stole, worn on top of the chasuble-alb, be the color of the Mass which is celebrated."[44] It is presumed that the color of the chasuble-alb is white.

In 1978, a description of this vestment was offered: "The chasuble-alb is a large, full-length chasuble-shaped vestment designed without sleeves. A chasuble would never be worn over it since it has the cut and appearance of a full chasuble."[45]

All concelebrants may, of course, wear chasubles. If this is done, their chasubles "should be simpler in their decoration than that of the principal celebrant."[46] The role of the one presider must never be obscured by concelebrants. "Only one bishop or one presbyter presides over the whole celebration. Furthermore, the position of the concelebrants should not usurp the positions nor limit the functioning of other liturgical ministers nor block the view of the assembly."[47]

"If a sufficient number of chasubles is not available, and in order to avoid the impression of two classes of concelebrants, it may be preferable for all the concelebrants to be vested in albs and stoles."[48]

In choosing vesture for concelebration, it is important to remember that "whatever vestments are used . . . they are a part of the total ritual experience and need . . . to be of good quality and design. . . . They should constitute a set of harmonious colors and dignified pattern."[49] It is "the color and form of the vestments and their difference from everyday clothing [that] call attention to the liturgical role of the concelebrants. Vestments are part of the ritual experience and the festive character of a liturgical celebration."[50]

Primarily for this reason, "priests may not concelebrate in ordinary clerical garb or by wearing the stole over the cassock or street clothing. Nor may priests of religious institutes concelebrate merely by placing a stole over their monastic cowl or habit."[51]

Deacons

"The dalmatic, worn over the alb and stole, is the vestment proper to the deacon. The deacon wears [the stole] over his left shoulder and drawn across the chest to the right side, where it is fastened."[52]

Other Ministers

Any "minister below the order of deacon may wear the alb or other vestment that is lawfully approved."[53] However, since the alb has become so associated through the course of history with the ministerial priesthood, another choice of vestment for non-ministerial persons may need to be made. The caution is not to separate other ministers from the rest of the community.

Altar and Ambo

At certain times, in order to create a festive environment, "vesture may . . . be used appropriately on an altar or ambo or other objects."[54] (Suggestions as to how this can be done are found in ch. 2, "The Altar Is Christ," and ch. 3, "The Table of the Word of God.") When clothing the altar and the ambo, the vesture should not be used as " 'frontals' or 'facades,' but as decorative covering which respects the integrity and totality of the particular object."[55]

Fabric

The fabric used in making vestments "should be chosen because of the quality of design, texture and color."[56] "Natural fabrics . . . may be used for making vestments; artificial fabrics that are in keeping with the dignity of the liturgy and the person wearing them may also be used."[57]

Colors

According to the December 1987 edition of the *Bishops' Committee on the Liturgy Newsletter* of the National Conference of Catholic Bishops,

. . . only those colors mentioned in the *General Instruction of the Roman Missal* (no. 308) and in the Appendix to the *General Instruction of the Roman Missal* (no. 308) have been approved by the National Conference of Catholic Bishops:

[1] *white* for the offices and Masses of the Easter and Christmas seasons, feasts and memorials of the Lord (other than of his passion), feasts and memorials of Mary, the angels, saints who were not martyrs, All Saints, John the Baptist (June 24), John the Evangelist (December 27), Chair of St. Peter (February 22), Conversion of St. Paul (January 25); in the United States white may also be used for offices and Masses for the dead;

[2] *red* for Passion (Palm) Sunday, Good Friday, Pentecost, celebrations of the Lord's passion, birthday feasts of the apostles and evangelists, celebrations of the martyrs;

[3] *green* for the offices and Masses of Ordinary Time;

[4] *violet* for the offices and Masses of the seasons of Advent and Lent, and for the dead;

[5] *black* (as well as violet and white) may be used for the offices and Masses for the dead;

[6] *rose* may be used on Gaudete Sunday (Third Sunday of Advent) and on Laetare Sunday (Fourth Sunday of Lent).[58]

The "variety in the color of the vestments is meant to give effective, outward expression to the specific character of the mysteries of the faith being celebrated and, in the course of the year, to a sense of progress in the Christian life."[59]

Even though other Churches use blue vestments during the season of Advent, "the NCCB has neither proposed nor approved the use of blue either for the season of Advent or for memorials and feasts of Mary, nor any other color."[60]

Banners

The respect for integrity and totality especially applies to the creation of banners, "temporary decoration for particular celebrations, feasts and seasons."[61] Probably nothing has been more abused since Vatican Council II than the indiscriminate use of banners. This is not to say that they should never be employed in a worship space.

"Banners and hangings of various sorts are both popular and appropriate, as long as the nature of these art forms are respected."[62] However, what comes to mind as a banner—a wall, altar, ambo, or standard hanging with words and signs pasted on it—is not what is prescribed in the liturgical books. According to *Environment and Art in Catholic Worship,* banners and hang-

ings "are creations of forms, colors, and textures, rather than signboards to which words must be attached."[63]

A banner or hanging is not created "to impress a slogan upon the minds of observers or deliver a verbal message."[64] Rather, a banner or a hanging is created "to appeal to the senses and thereby create an atmosphere and a mood."[65] If this principle is kept in mind, many of the banners and hangings in worship spaces will need to be removed.

Conclusion

In general, the reverence shown to the vesture which clothes the ministers and the church flows from the theology of vesture as found in the documents of the Church. This theology of vesture should inform praxis. In other words, the theology of vesture should be seen in its created form in the vesture employed during worship.

Notes

1. CSL, no. 7.
2. DMLP, no. 2.
3. DCCBS.
4. DCC, no. 10.
5. Ibid., no. 11.
6. IWEM, no. 11.
7. GIRM, nos. 1–3.
8. Ibid., nos. 3–4.
9. EACW, no. 29.
10. GIRM, no. 297.
11. Ibid.
12. Cf. EACW, no. 93.
13. EACW, no. 60.
14. Ibid.
15. Ibid., no. 93.
16. Ibid.
17. Ibid., no. 84.
18. GIRM, no. 297.
19. EACW, no. 93.
20. Ibid.
21. GIRM, no. 307.
22. Ibid., no. 309.
23. DCC, no. 11.
24. Ibid., no. 10.
25. IWEM, no. 11.
26. Ibid.
27. Cf. DMLP, no. 2.
28. GIRM, no. 298.
29. EACW, no. 14.
30. Ibid., no. 15.
31. Cf. EACW, no. 15.
32. GIRM, no. 287.
33. EACW, no. 85.
34. Ibid., no. 86.
35. Ibid., no. 87.
36. Ibid., no. 94.
37. GIRM, no. 306.
38. EACW, no. 86.
39. Ibid., no. 94.
40. GIRM, no. 302.
41. Ibid., no. 299.
42. Ibid., no. 303.
43. Ibid., no. 161.

44. BCLN 13 (May–June 1977) 69.
45. BCLN 14 (April–May 1978) 116.
46. BCLN 23 (September–October 1987) 37.
47. Ibid., 36.
48. Ibid., 37.
49. BCLN 16 (November 1980) 235.
50. BCLN 23 (September–October 1987) 36.
51. Ibid., 36–37.
52. GIRM, nos. 300 and 302.
53. GIRM, no. 301.
54. EACW, no. 95.
55. Ibid.
56. Ibid., no. 95.
57. GIRM, no. 305.
58. BCLN 23 (December 1987) 48; cf. GIRM, no. 308.
59. GIRM, no. 307.
60. BCLN 23 (December 1987) 48.
61. EACW, no. 100.
62. Ibid.
63. Ibid.
64. Ibid.
65. Ibid.

Chapter 9

The Holy Oils and Their Repository

Ecclesial Documents

The norm of active participation concerning the holy oils and their repository is fleshed out in two documents: (1) the "Order for the Blessing of a Repository for the Holy Oils" in the *Book of Blessings* and (2) the "Rites of the Blessing of Oils and Consecrating the Chrism" in the Sacramentary.

The "Order for the Blessing of a Repository for the Holy Oils" within Mass states that "after the gospel reading, the celebrant in the homily, based on the sacred text and pertinent to the particular place and the people involved, explains the meaning of the celebration."[1] In the "Order of Blessing Within a Celebration of the Word of God," the rubrics declare that "as circumstances suggest, the minister may give those present a brief explanation of the biblical text, so that they may understand through faith the meaning of the celebration."[2]

The Introduction to the "Rites of the Blessing of Oils and Consecrating the Chrism" states: "The bishop is to be considered as the high priest of his flock. The life in Christ of his faithful is in some way derived from and dependent upon the bishop."[3] From this understanding, then, "the chrism Mass is one of the principal expressions of the fullness of the bishop's priesthood and signifies the close unity of the priests with him."[4]

Because priests minister to the people of God through the use of the holy oils, the people themselves participate in this celebration.

"The newly baptized are anointed and confirmed with the chrism consecrated by the bishop. Catechumens are prepared and disposed for bap-

152

tism with the second oil. And the sick are anointed in their illness with the third oil."[5]

Our consideration here is the theology of the holy oils and their repository found in the documents of the Church and the praxis which should flow from this theology. Therefore, after exploring the theology of the holy oils as presented by Vatican Council II, praxis, which either fosters or impedes active participation, will be examined.

It must be noted that the blessing of a repository for the holy oils usually takes places within the rite of a dedication of a church. "When a church is to be consecrated to God or is to be blessed by use of the rite for the dedication of a church, everything in the church, except the altar, is regarded as blessed and erected in virtue of the rite of dedication or blessing, so that no further rite is needed."[6] However, "there are certain blessings that have particular significance and importance in the life of the ecclesial community."[7] Since the focus is on the repository for the holy oils, only the texts that deal with it and the holy oils will be treated.

Theology of the Holy Oils

Oil of Catechumens

The first of three oils used in the celebration of the rites of the Church is that called the "oil of catechumens." It is usually "blessed by the bishop with the other oils during the chrism Mass" on Holy Thursday[8] although "in the case of the baptism of adults . . . priests have the faculty to bless the oil of catechumens before the anointing in the designated stage of the catechumenate."[9] During the catechumenate "the rite of anointing the catechumens, through the use of the oil of catechumens, may be celebrated wherever this seems beneficial or desirable."[10] The "rite of anointing may be celebrated several times during the course of the catechumenate."[11]

The *Rite of Christian Initiation of Adults* makes clear the significance of this anointing. "The anointing with oil symbolizes [the catechumen's] need for God's help and strength so that, undeterred by the bonds of the past and overcoming the opposition of the devil, they will forthrightly take the step of professing their faith and will hold fast to it unfalteringly throughout their lives."[12]

The prayer of blessing of the oil of catechumens, which is given in the *Rite of Christian Initiation of Adults*, further emphasizes the strengthening significance of the rite of anointing. The priest calls upon "God, source of strength and defender of . . . people" to bless the oil and to "strengthen the catechumens who will be anointed with it." The prayer also petitions that the catechumens be granted God's "wisdom to understand the Gospel more deeply" and God's "strength to accept the challenges of Christian life."[13]

As each catechumen is anointed with the oil, the celebrant says:

> We anoint you with the oil of salvation
> in the name of Christ our Savior.
> May he strengthen you with his power,
> who lives and reigns for ever and ever.[14]

Thus, once again, the emphasis is placed on strengthening the catechumen as he or she prepares for the day of his or her baptism.

Before children are baptized, they are anointed with the oil of catechumens while the words quoted above are said by the celebrant.[15] The *Rite of Baptism for Children* is a condensed form of the *Rite of Christian Initiation of Adults*.

The emphasis on strengthening the catechumens is also found in the "Rites of the Blessing of Oils and Consecrating the Chrism": "By the oil of catechumens the effect of the baptismal exorcisms is extended. Before they go to the font of life to be reborn the candidates for baptism are strengthened to renounce sin and the devil."[16]

In the prayer of blessing, the bishop asks the Lord God to bless the oil

and give wisdom and strength
to all who are anointed with it
in preparation for their baptism.
Bring them a deeper understanding of the gospel,
help them to accept the challenge of Christian living,
and lead them to the joy of new birth
in the family of your Church.[17]

When a new repository for the holy oils is to be blessed, one of the general intercessions is "that those who are anointed with the oil of catechumens may resist sin and temptation and embrace Christ wholeheartedly."[18] If the blessing takes place within a celebration of the word of God, among the words with which the minister prepares those present for the blessing are these which focus on the oil of catechumens: "By the anointing with oil . . . the catechumens are empowered to resist Satan and to reject sin and evil."[19]

The oil of catechumens, then, serves as an ointment of strengthening for those who are anointed with it. It symbolizes their need for God's help and strength, and it empowers them to resist Satan and reject sin and evil.

Oil of the Sick

The second of three oils used in the celebration of the rites of the Church is that called the "oil of the sick." "The oil of the sick is ordinarily blessed by the bishop on Holy Thursday."[20] "The oil used for anointing the sick must be blessed for this purpose by the bishop or by a priest who has this faculty," or "in case of true necessity, any priest" may bless the oil.[21]

Pastoral Care of the Sick: Rites of Anointing and Viaticum explains that "the practice of anointing the sick with oil signifies healing, strengthening, and the presence of the Spirit."[22]

The healing aspect of the rite of anointing is emphasized in the prayers of blessing of the oil of the sick, of which the first choice in the *Pastoral Care of the Sick* is the same as that prayed by the bishop during the Chrism Mass. After addressing the "God of all consolation," the bishop or priest says:

You chose and sent your Son to heal the world. . . .
Make this oil a remedy for all who are anointed with it;
heal them in body, in soul, and in spirit,
and deliver them from every affliction.[23]

The *Pastoral Care of the Sick* provides two other prayers of blessing for use by the priest. In one of these optional three-part prayers, which with a slightly different conclusion can also be used as a prayer of thanksgiving over oil that has already been blessed, the priest prays:

> Praise to you, God, the only-begotten Son.
> You humbled yourself to share in our humanity and you heal our infirmities.[24]

In the conclusion he asks God to come to the aid of his people and to sanctify the oil "which has been set apart for healing" his people. He asks that "the prayer of faith and the anointing with oil" will free the sick "from every affliction."[25]

The second of these two other prayers of blessing for the oil of the sick is very short.

> Bless, Lord, your gift of oil
> and our brother/sister
> that it may bring him/her relief.[26]

Both the healing and the strengthening aspects of the anointing of the sick are emphasized in the words of instruction given to those persons participating in a blessing of a new repository for the holy oils within a celebration of the word of God, as provided in the *Book of Blessings*. The minister reminds the people that "by anointing with oil, the sick are strengthened and healed."[27] According to the *Pastoral Care of the Sick*, "the sick person is strengthened to fight against the physically and spiritually debilitating effects of illness."[28] And the introduction to the "Rites of the Blessing of Oils and Consecrating the Chrism" declares, "By the use of the oil of the sick, . . . the sick receive a remedy for the illness of mind and body, so that they may have strength to bear suffering and resist evil and obtain forgiveness of sins."[29]

The third aspect of the anointing of the sick—"the presence of the Spirit"[30]—is found particularly in the first prayer of blessing of the oil. "The prayer for blessing the oil of the sick reminds us . . . that the oil of anointing is the sacramental sign of the presence, power, and grace of the Holy Spirit."[31] In this prayer the priest or bishop asks the "God of all consolation" to

> graciously listen to our prayer of faith:
> send the power of your Holy Spirit, the Consoler,
> into this precious oil, this soothing ointment,
> this rich gift, this fruit of the earth.[32]

In the second possible prayer of blessing of the oil of the sick found in the *Pastoral Care of the Sick,* the priest prays:

> Praise to you, God, the Holy Spirit, the Consoler.
> Your unfailing power gives us strength
> in our bodily weakness.[33]

The sacramental form of the rite is echoed in this prayer:

> Through this holy anointing
> may the Lord in his love and mercy help you
> with the grace of the Holy Spirit.[34]

Finally, all three aspects of the anointing of the sick are summed up in the last of the general intercessions provided for the blessing of a new repository for the holy oils. The minister prays "that those who are anointed with the oil of the sick may be strengthened, comforted, and healed by the grace of the Holy Spirit."[35] Thus, the oil of the sick serves as an ointment of healing, strengthening, and comfort in the presence of the Holy Spirit for those who are ill.

Chrism Oil

The last of three oils used in the celebration of the rites of the Church is that called the "chrism," from which the Mass within which it is consecrated takes its name. "The Christian liturgy has assimilated [the] Old Testament usage of anointing kings, priests, and prophets with consecratory oil because the name of Christ, whom they prefigured, means 'the anointed of the Lord.'"[36] "The consecration of the chrism belongs to the bishop alone."[37]

The Introduction to the "Rites of the Blessing of Oils and Consecrating the Chrism" makes clear the significance of the anointing with chrism: "Chrism is a sign: by baptism Christians are plunged into the paschal mystery of Christ; they die with him, are buried with him, and rise with him; they are sharers in his royal and prophetic priesthood. By confirmation Christians receive the spiritual anointing of the Spirit who is given to them."[38]

Two forms of the prayer for consecrating the chrism are given. The first recalls the beginning of creation, when "the earth produced fruit-bearing trees." It is "from the fruit of the olive tree" that chrism is made.[39] A reference to the "olive branch" brought to Noah after the Flood follows. "Now the waters of baptism wash away . . . sins . . . , and by the anointing with olive oil [God makes people] radiant with . . . joy."[40]

The baptismal theme is continued in the next Old Testament reference, the action of Moses first washing his brother, Aaron, and then "anointing him priest." The prayer declares that this "foreshadowed greater things to come"—namely, the sending of the Spirit "in the form of a dove and . . . the witness of [God's] own voice [when he] declared [Jesus] to be [his] only, well-beloved Son." In this "the prophecy of David" was fulfilled, "that Christ would be anointed with the oil of gladness beyond his fellow men."[41]

Then, the bishop prays:

> Fill [the oil] with the power of your Holy Spirit
> through Christ your Son.
> It is from him that chrism takes its name
> and with chrism your have anointed
> for yourself priests and kings,
> prophets and martyrs.
>
> Make this chrism a sign of life and salvation
> for those who are to be born again in the waters of baptism . . .
> and when they are anointed with this holy oil
> make them temples of your glory,
> radiant with the goodness of life
> that has its source in you.[42]

The emphasis on the royal, priestly, prophetic role of baptism is emphasized once again in the prayer, when the bishop prays:

> Through this sign of chrism
> grant them royal, priestly, and prophetic honor,
> and clothe them with incorruption.
> Let this be indeed the chrism of salvation
> for those who will be born again of water and the Holy Spirit.[43]

The baptismal emphasis of this first consecratory prayer of the chrism is carried through in the *Rite of Christian Initiation of Adults*. This document declares that "the anointing with chrism is a sign of the royal priesthood of the baptized and that they are now numbered in the company of the people of God."[44] This anointing may take place after baptism, as it does for children, or, preferably, it takes place during confirmation, which "in accord with the ancient practice followed in the Roman liturgy, adults are not to be baptized without receiving confirmation immediately afterward, unless some serious reason stands in the way."[45]

The reason given for this is that "the conjunction of the two celebrations signifies the unity of the paschal mystery, the close link between the mission of the Son and the outpouring of the Holy Spirit, and the connection between the two sacraments through which the Son and the Holy Spirit come with the Father to those who are baptized."[46]

In the case of children and in the case of adults when confirmation is to be delayed, before the newly baptized are anointed with chrism the celebrant prays:

> The God of power and Father of our Lord Jesus Christ
> has freed you from sin
> and brought you to new life
> through water and the Holy Spirit.
> He now anoints you with the chrism of salvation,
> so that, united with his people,
> you may remain for ever a member of Christ
> who is Priest, Prophet, and King.[47]

The prayer for children differs slightly but emphasizes the same baptismal themes as the celebrant says: "God the Father of our Lord Jesus Christ has freed you from sin, given you a new birth by water and the Holy Spirit, and welcomed you into his holy people. He now anoints you with the chrism of salvation. As Christ was anointed Priest, Prophet, and King, so may you live always as a member of his body, sharing everlasting life."[48]

When a new repository for the holy oils is to be blessed, in one of the general intercessions the minister prays "that those who are sealed with holy chrism in baptism and confirmation may live their faith with confidence."[49] In the words used to prepare those present for the blessing within a celebration of the word of God, the minister says, "By the anointing with oil . . . the baptized are sealed with the gifts of the Spirit."[50]

This sealing aspect of the anointing with chrism oil is found in the celebration of confirmation, when the bishop or priest "dips his right thumb in the chrism and makes the sign of the cross on the forehead of the one to be confirmed as he says: N., be sealed with the Gift of the Holy Spirit."[51]

In preparation for this sealing, the newly baptized, those "born again in Christ by baptism," are told that they "have become members of Christ and of his priestly people." They "are to share in the outpouring of the Holy Spirit . . . , the Spirit sent by the Lord upon his apostles at Pentecost and given by them and their successors to the baptized."[52]

"The promised strength of the Holy Spirit . . . will make" the newly baptized "more like Christ" and help them "to be witnesses to his suffering, death, and resurrection. It will strengthen [them] to be active members of the Church and to build up the Body of Christ in faith and love."[53]

After all pray "to God . . . that he will pour out the Holy Spirit on [the] newly baptized to strengthen them with his gifts and anoint them to be more like Christ, the Son of God,"[54] the bishop or priest with "his hands outstretched over the entire group of those to be confirmed"—the sign of calling down the Holy Spirit—says:

> All-powerful God, Father of our Lord Jesus Christ,
> by water and the Holy Spirit
> you freed your sons and daughters from sin
> and gave them new life.
>
> Send your Holy Spirit upon them
> to be their helper and guide.
>
> Give them the spirit of wisdom and understanding,
> the spirit of right judgment and courage,
> the spirit of knowledge and reverence.
> Fill them with the spirit of wonder and awe in your presence.[55]

The second prayer for consecrating the chrism, while it places an emphasis on baptismal themes, points toward the other people and things that are anointed with chrism. A brief reference is made to "the Old Covenant" in which the Father gave his people "a glimpse of the power of [the] holy oil," which, "when the fullness of time had come," he "brought that mystery to perfection in the life of [the] Lord Jesus Christ."[56]

A reference to the paschal mystery, the "suffering, dying, and rising to life" of Jesus, who sent the "Spirit to fill the Church with every gift needed to complete [God's] saving work"[57] is made. It is "through the sign of holy chrism" that the Father dispenses his "life and love" to people. "By anointing them with the Spirit, [he] strengthens all who have been reborn in baptism. Through that anointing" he transforms "them into the likeness of Christ" and gives "them a share in his royal, priestly, and prophetic work."[58]

After asking that the Father make the "mixture of oil and perfume"—the chrism oil—"a sign and source" of his blessing, the bishop prays to the Father: "Pour out the gifts of your Holy Spirit on our brothers and sisters who will be anointed with [the oil]. Let the splendor of holiness shine on the world from every place and thing signed with this oil." Finally, the bishop prays, "Father, . . . through this sign of your anointing . . . grant increase to your Church."[59]

This second form of consecrating the chrism points toward the use of chrism oil in other rites of the Church. When a priest is ordained, the palms of his hands are anointed. While doing this, the bishop says:

> The Father anointed our Lord Jesus Christ
> through the power of the Holy Spirit.
> May Jesus preserve you to sanctify the Christian people
> and to offer sacrifice to God.[60]

When a bishop is ordained, the principal consecrator anoints him with chrism oil on the head and says:

> God has brought you to share the high priesthood of Christ.
> May he pour out on you the mystical anointing
> and enrich you with spiritual blessings.[61]

In the introductory words provided for the order of blessing a new repository within a celebration of the word of God, the minister, instructing those participating, reminds them of the anointing of priests and bishops with chrism by saying, "By the anointing with oil . . . the ministers of the Church are sanctified in God's service."[62] Also, in one of the general intercessions in the same *Book of Blessings,* the minister prays "that those ordained to the service of God and the Church may be ministers of mercy, compassion, and love."[63]

When a new church building is dedicated, the altar and the walls of the church are anointed with chrism. Before the anointing, the bishop says:

> We now anoint this altar and this building.
> May God in his power make them holy,
> visible signs of the mystery of Christ and his Church.[64]

"In virtue of the anointing with chrism the altar becomes a symbol of Christ who, before all others, is and is called 'The Anointed One'; for the Father anointed him with the Holy Spirit and constituted him the High Priest who on the altar of his body would offer the sacrifice of his life for the salvation of all; the anointing of the church signifies that it is given over entirely and perpetually to Christian worship."[65] A more detailed description of the anointing of the altar and the walls of the church can be found in Chapter 2, "The Altar Is Christ."

In *The Dedication of a Church and an Altar: A Theological Commentary,* Ignazio M. Calabuig summarizes the meaning of this dual anointing with chrism: "If in the building dedicated to worship the altar is Christ, the stones holding up the walls are Christians (see 1 Pet 2:5). As the Head was anointed with the Spirit, so are the members in the sacraments; as the altar was anointed, so are the stones."[66]

The anointing with chrism oil, then, represents the fact that a person has become another Christ; he or she has become another "anointed one." In this capacity, in baptism the person shares in the royal, priestly, prophetic role of Christ. In confirmation he or she is sealed with the Gift of the Holy Spirit. In the ordination to priesthood a man's hands are anointed to sanctify and to offer sacrifice. When a man is ordained to the episcopacy, his head is anointed to indicate that he now shares in the high priesthood of Christ. And the anointing of the altar and walls of a new church building illustrate how the members of the Church are anointed with the Spirit in the sacraments, which are celebrated in the church. Whoever and whatever is anointed with chrism is "Christed."

Oils in General

In summary, then, the theology of the holy oils is found in their use. "God manifests his grace through the sacramental signs he has entrusted to his Church,"[67] the *Book of Blessings* declares. When using the holy oils, the Church prays that "through the use of these holy oils may God's grace be poured forth always upon the Church."[68]

The prayer of blessing for a new repository for the holy oils or for the vessels used for storing the oils brings together the theology of each of the oils. The celebrant prays that the "gracious and loving God," who "anointed priests, prophets, and kings of old with the oil of gladness" and who infuses the "Church with the gifts of the Holy Spirit" and heals, comforts, and sanctifies "those anointed with oil" in his name, will "let this repository (these vessels) remind [all] always of [his] sacramental mysteries."[69]

Then, he names the oils and prays:

> May the holy oils kept here,
> the oil of the sick, the oil of catechumens, and holy chrism,
> confirm our unity in faith and prayer with our bishop
> and with all the members of your Church,
> and be effective signs of the love
> that you pour forth into our hearts.[70]

Praxis

From this understanding of the theology of the holy oils, there flows a definite practice. As with all the revisions inaugurated by Vatican Council II, the theological background is given as a reason for the praxis which follows.

The Repository for the Holy Oils

Environment and Art in Catholic Worship reminds us that "every word, gesture, movement, object, appointment must be real in the sense that it is our own. It must come from the deepest understanding of ourselves."[71] This same point is emphasized in the *Book of Blessings:* "The Church has always sought to ensure that all those things that are involved in any way in divine worship should be worthy, becoming, and beautiful; that they first be blessed, and then kept exclusively for sacred celebrations, and never turned to commonplace uses. It is the Church's intention to maintain this practice. Consequently, those objects that through a blessing are set aside for divine worship are to be treated with reverence by all and to be put only to their proper use, never profaned."[72]

Therefore, care must be given to the design and shape of the repository in which are kept "the oils used for the celebration of the sacraments of initiation, holy orders, and the anointing of the sick." It is "according to ancient tradition" that these oils are "reverently reserved in a special place in the church."[73]

In older churches that have a small box in either one of the walls of the sanctuary or in the sacristy marked *Olea Sanctae*—"Holy Oils"—the three oils should be stored there. In newer churches a repository may need to be installed. In this case, the possibility of preparing a glass case either mounted to a wall or mounted to a shelf should be explored. "The repository should be secure and be protected by a lock."[74] However, this does not exclude the construction of a repository that is visible.

The repository should be placed in the baptistery in churches that have one. In those without a baptistery, the repository should be located near the place where baptisms take place, since two of the three oils are used in the celebration of this sacrament. If this is not possible, some other appropriate place in the church should be chosen. However, because of the importance of the oils, it does seem that they should not be kept in a cabinet or a drawer in the sacristy but rather in a prominent place in the church where all members can be reminded of their repeated anointings, which make them other Christs.

Containers for the Holy Oils

The *Book of Blessings* states, "The vessels used to hold the holy oils should be worthy of their function and be closed in such a way as to prevent the oils from being spilled and to insure that they remain fresh."[75] *Environment and Art in Catholic Worship* also emphasizes the suitability of the vessels for the oils: "All other vessels and implements used in the liturgical celebration should be of such quality and design that they speak of the importance of the ritual action. . . . Vessels for holy oils . . . are presented to the assembly in one way or another and speak well or ill of the deed in which the assembly is engaged."[76]

The rite of the *Pastoral Care of the Sick* emphasizes the importance of the containers for the oil of the sick. "If the priest uses oil that has already been blessed (either by the bishop or by a priest), he brings it with him in the vessel in which it is kept. This vessel, made of suitable material, should be clean and should contain sufficient oil (soaked in cotton for convenience). In this case, after celebrating the sacrament the priest returns the vessel to the place where it is kept with proper respect."[77]

With these guidelines in place, it would seem that there are a number of possible solutions for containers for the holy oils. First, small glass flagons might be used for the oil of the catechumens and for the chrism. Each should be different in design in order to indicate the oil which each contains. When used, the oil could be poured directly from the flagon onto the person being anointed, or it could be poured into a small glass bowl into which the minister can dip his thumb.

Second, small pottery flagons might be used. Like the glass, these should be different in size, shape, and design to easily distinguish the oils from each other. With a stopper fitted with cork, the oil of the sick could be kept in such a container and easily transported without danger of spilling. Instead of glass bowls, pottery bowls which match their respective flagons could be used for celebrations involving anointings.

Third, pouring either the oil of catechumens or the chrism into a traditional metal oil stock which has been stuffed with cotton does not seem to illustrate or highlight the importance of the oils, as has been seen in the documents of the Church. If no other means can be found, then the oil of the sick might be transported this way. However, with the option to bless the oil of the sick during the celebration of anointing, the priest "may bring the unblessed oil with him, or the family of the sick person may prepare the oil in a suitable vessel."[78]

In this case, a small oil stock might be convenient, but it does not fulfill this directive: "If the anointing is to be an effective sacramental symbol, there should be a generous use of oil so that it will be seen and felt by the sick person as a sign of the Spirit's healing and strengthening presence."[79]

Because of the importance of the vessels which contain the oil, the Introduction to the "Order for the Blessing of a Repository for the Holy Oils" in the *Book of Blessings* states that the "order may be used for blessing a repository for the holy oils or blessing the vessels in which the oils are stored. The celebration may take place during Mass or a celebration of the word of God."[80]

Making the Oils

The "Rites of the Blessing of Oils and Consecrating the Chrism" makes it clear that "the matter proper for the sacraments is olive oil or, according to circumstances, other plant oil."[81] *Pastoral Care of the Sick* emphasizes this same point: "The matter proper for the sacrament is olive oil or, according to circumstances, other oil derived from plants."[82] "Chrism is made of oil and perfumes or other sweet smelling matter."[83]

Since olive oil is the preferred matter for the oils and since it is easy to get, this seems to be the obvious choice. In preparing the chrism, liquid balsam, a sweet smelling perfume which mixes with olive oil, is available from most supply stores. If another type of perfume is added, it should mix with the olive oil. The fragrance of the chrism should set it apart from the other oils, so that when one is anointed with it the aroma fills the church. "It is not desirable to wipe off the oil after the anointing."[84]

"The preparation of the chrism may take place privately before the rite of consecration or may be done by the bishop during the liturgical service."[85]

Replacing the Holy Oils

In general, "each year when the bishop blesses the oils and consecrates the chrism, the pastor should see that the old oils are properly disposed of by burning and that they are replaced by the newly blessed oils."[86] However, since the priest may bless the oil of catechumens and the oil of the sick within their respective rites, "he should make sure that the oil remains fit for use and should replenish it from time to time, either yearly when the bishop blesses the oil on Holy Thursday or more frequently if necessary."[87] If a priest blesses oil while in the home of a sick person, "any of the oil [that] is left after the celebration of the sacrament [of the anointing of the sick] . . . should be absorbed in cotton and burned.''[88]

The usual way of properly disposing of the old oils is to pour them over cotton and burn them. This mixture of oil and cotton could be used as part of the fire for Holy Saturday. Another way of disposing of the old oils is to pour them into a large burning sanctuary lamp, where they will be burned by the candle. Keeping old oils in bottles stored on shelves or in drawers in sacristies does not give the oils the respect called for in the documents of the Church.

Conclusion

In general, the reverence shown to the repository for the holy oils flows from the theology of the oils found in the documents of the Church. The theology of the oils should inform praxis, which includes anything connected with any of the rites of the Church that involve anointing with oil. Every Christian must remember that ''the life in Christ of [the] faithful is in some way derived and dependent upon the bishop.''[89] The Chrism Mass, during which the holy oils are blessed and the chrism is consecrated, ''is one of the principal expressions of the fullness of the bishop's priesthood and signifies the close unity of the priests with him.''[90]

This unity flows out into the parish, ''set up locally under a pastor who takes the place of a bishop. . . . Therefore, the liturgical life of the parish and its relation to the bishop must be fostered in the spirit and practice of the laity and clergy. Efforts must be made to encourage a sense of community within the parish.''[91] The Christian's purpose exists in participating in worship in his or her parish and thus ''in some way'' representing ''the visible Church constituted throughout the world.''[92]

Notes

1. BB, no. 1130.
2. Ibid, no. 1140.
3. TS, RBOCC, no. 1.
4. Ibid.
5. Ibid.
6. BB, no. 1078.
7. Ibid., no. 1079.
8. TS, RBOCC, no. 7.

9. Ibid.
10. RCIA, no. 98.
11. Ibid., no. 100.
12. Ibid., no. 99.
13. RCIA, no. 102.
14. Ibid., no. 103.
15. Cf. RBC, no. 50.
16. TS, RBOCC, no. 2.
17. Ibid., no. 22.
18. BB, nos. 1131 and 1141.
19. Ibid., no. 1136.
20. PCS, no. 21.
21. TS, RBOCC, no. 8; cf. PCS, no. 21.
22. PCS, no. 107.
23. Ibid., no. 123; TS, RBOCC, no. 20.
24. PCS, no. 140.
25. Ibid.
26. Ibid., no. 248.
27. BB, no. 1136.
28. PCS, no. 107.
29. TS, RBOCC, no. 2.
30. PCS, no. 107.
31. Ibid.
32. Ibid., no. 123; TS, RBOCC, no. 20.
33. PCS, no. 140.
34. PCS, no. 25.
35. BB, nos. 1131 and 1141.
36. TS, RBOCC, no. 2.
37. Ibid., no. 6.
38. Ibid., no. 2.
39. Ibid., no. 25.
40. Ibid.
41. Ibid.
42. Ibid.
43. Ibid.
44. RCIA, no. 214; cf. RBC, no. 18.
45. RCIA, no. 215.
46. Ibid.
47. Ibid., no. 228.
48. RBC, no. 62.
49. BB, nos. 1131 and 1141.
50. Ibid., no. 1136.
51. RCIA, no. 235.
52. Ibid., no. 233.
53. Ibid.

54. Ibid.
55. Ibid., no. 234.
56. RBOCC, no. 25.
57. Ibid.
58. Ibid.
59. Ibid.
60. RP:OP, no. 24.
61. RP:OB, no. 28.
62. BB, no. 1136.
63. Ibid., nos. 1131 and 1141.
64. DCA, "Dedication of a Church," ch. 2, no. 64.
65. Ibid., no. 16.
66. DCA:C, 26.
67. BB, no. 1136.
68. Ibid.
69. Ibid., nos. 1132, 1143, and 1149.
70. Ibid.
71. EACW, no. 14.
72. BB, no. 1076.
73. Ibid., no. 1125.
74. Ibid.
75. Ibid., no. 1126.
76. EACW, no. 97.
77. PCS, no. 22.
78. Ibid.
79. Ibid., no. 107.
80. BB, no. 1128.
81. TS, RBOCC, no. 3.
82. PCS, no. 20.
83. TS, RBOCC, no. 4.
84. PCS, no. 107.
85. TS, RBOCC, no. 5.
86. BB, no. 1127.
87. PCS, no. 22.
88. Ibid.
89. TS, RBOCC, no. 1.
90. Ibid.
91. CSL, no. 42.
92. Ibid.

Chapter 10

The Place of Reconciliation

Ecclesial Documents

The norm of active participation concerning the place for reconciliation is fleshed out in two documents: (1) the "Order for the Blessing of a New Confessional," which is found in the *Book of Blessings,* and (2) *The Rite of Penance.*

The introduction to the "Order for the Blessing of a New Confessional" states that "the practice of reserving a special place in churches for the celebration of the sacrament of reconciliation is a clear expression of the truth that sacramental confession and absolution constitute a liturgical action which involves the entire body of the Church and is intended to renew the participation of the faithful in the Church's offering of the sacrifice of Christ."[1]

The Rite of Penance also makes it clear that "the whole Church, as a priestly people, acts in different ways in the work of reconciliation which has been entrusted to it by the Lord."[2] The document explains that "not only does the Church call sinners to repentance by preaching the word of God, but it also intercedes for them and helps penitents with maternal care and solicitude to acknowledge and admit their sins and so obtain the mercy of God who alone can forgive sins. Furthermore, the Church becomes the instrument of the conversion and absolution of the penitent through the ministry entrusted by Christ to the apostles and their successors."[3]

In particular, "the Church exercises the ministry of the sacrament of penance through bishops and presbyters. By preaching God's word they call the faithful to conversion; in the name of Christ and by the power of the Holy Spirit they declare and grant the forgiveness of sins."[4]

However, "the acts of the penitent in the celebration of the sacrament are of the greatest importance. When with proper dispositions he [or she] approaches this saving remedy instituted by Christ and confesses his [or her] sins, he [or she] shares by his [or her] actions in the sacrament itself. Thus the faithful Christian, as he [or she] experiences and proclaims the mercy of God in his [or her] life, celebrates with the priest the liturgy by which the Church continually renews itself."[5]

Our consideration here is the theology of sin and penance found in the documents of the Church and the praxis which should flow from this theology. Therefore, after exploring the theology of sin and penance as presented by Vatican Council II, praxis, which either fosters or impedes active participation, will be examined.

It must be noted that the blessing of a new confessional usually takes places within the rite of a dedication of a church. "When a church is dedicated or blessed, all the appointments that are already in place are considered to be blessed along with the church. But when . . . the confessional [is] newly installed or renovated, there is an opportunity to teach the faithful the importance of such [an] appointment by means of the celebration of a blessing."[6] Since the focus is on the place of reconciliation, only the texts that deal with it will be treated.

Theology of Sin and Penance

Briefly stated, the Church believes that "every sin is an offense against God which disrupts . . . friendship with him."[7] But "by the hidden and loving mystery of God's design men [and women] are joined together in the bonds of supernatural solidarity, so much so that the sin of one harms the others. . . . Penance always entails reconciliation with [the] brothers and sisters who are always harmed by . . . sins."[8]

The Rite of Penance states this clearly in the introduction: "Men [and women] frequently join together to commit injustice. It is thus only fitting that they should help each other in doing penance so that freed from sin by the grace of Christ they may work with all men [and women] of good will for justice and peace in the world."[9]

"The follower of Christ who has sinned but who has been moved by the Holy Spirit to come to the sacrament of penance should above all be converted to God with his [or her] whole heart. This inner conversion of heart embraces sorrow for sin and the intent to lead a new life. It is expressed through confession made to the Church, due satisfaction, and amendment of life. God grants pardon for sin through the Church, which works by the ministry of priests."[10]

Reconciliation as an action of God through the Church is emphasized in the words of absolution prayed by the priest or bishop. First, God is called the "Father of mercies," who through the paschal mystery—"the death and resurrection of his Son"—"has reconciled the world to himself and sent the Holy Spirit . . . for the forgiveness of sins." Second, it is "through the ministry of the Church" that God gives "pardon and peace."[11]

Also, the emphasis on the communal nature of sin and the communal aspect of forgiveness is found in the "act of penance or satisfaction" which the priest "imposes . . . on the penitent." *The Rite of Penance* makes it clear that "this should serve not only to make up for the past but also to help [the penitent] to begin a new life and provide him [or her] an antidote to weakness." The introduction suggests that penance "take the form of prayer, self-denial, and especially service of one's neighbor and works of mercy. These will underline the fact that sin and its forgiveness have a social aspect."[12]

The instruction given by the priest to the faithful when a new confessional is to be blessed also emphasizes these same points. The priest says: "The rite of blessing in which our faith leads us to take part moves us to learn that again and again we should thank God, who shows his almighty power most of all when in mercy he pardons our sins. We come to this confessional as sinners and we leave forgiven and restored to grace, because of the ministry of reconciliation that Christ Jesus has entrusted to his Church. Out of Christ's goodness those who are weighed down by sin are relieved of their burden when they come to the confessional; those who come here with the stains of evil upon them go away cleansed, washed in the blood of the Lamb."[13]

The intercessions provided for this rite form a litany of thanksgiving to God, "the almighty Father, who through the death and resurrection of his Son, in the power of the Holy Spirit, has delivered us from the dominion of darkness and forgiven us all our sins."[14]

The first intercession blesses the Lord "who has given [his] Son for . . . sins, so that [he] might snatch [people] from the power of darkness and bring [them] into the light and peace of [the] kingdom."[15]

The second intercession blesses the Lord, "who through the Holy Spirit rids [people's] conscience of the works of death."[16]

In the third intercession, the Lord is blessed for having given the Church "the keys of the kingdom so that the gates of . . . mercy may open wide to all."[17]

The last intercession declares, "Blessed are you, O Lord, who always accomplish great and wonderful deeds in the ministry of reconciliation, so that those whom you pardon may one day reach eternal life."[18]

The prayer of blessing, which is also the concluding prayer for the intercessions, reminds all sinners that it is "out of justice" that God corrects, "out of compassion" that God forgives, that God's ways "are always marked by mercy," his chastisement keeps people "from perishing forever," and his forbearance gives people "time to correct [their] ways."[19]

In summary, then, sin is understood as corporate evil. Penance, the gift of God's mercy, compassion, chastisement, and forbearance must be a corporate activity. Reconciliation takes place through the ministry of the whole Church. Such an understanding must influence the place where the sacrament of penance is celebrated and reconciliation takes place.

Praxis

From this understanding of the theology of sin and penance, there flows a definite practice. As with all the revisions inaugurated by Vatican Council II, the theological background is given as a reason for the praxis which follows.

The Reconciliation Chapel

The Rite of Penance states that "the sacrament of penance is celebrated in the place and location prescribed by law."[20] The Code of Canon Law states that "the proper place to hear sacramental confessions is a church or an oratory."[21]

The Code of Canon Law also states that "the conference of bishops is to issue norms concerning the confessional, seeing to it that confessionals with a fixed grille between penitent and confessor are always located in an open area so that the faithful who wish to make use of them may do so freely."[22]

Immediately following the issuance of *The Rite of Penance*, the bishops of the United States decreed that "small chapels or rooms of reconciliation be provided in which penitents might choose to confess their sins and seek sacramental reconciliation through an informal face-to-face exchange with the priest, with the opportunity for appropriate spiritual counsel."[23]

In the same decree, the United States bishops also stated that "such chapels or rooms [should] be designed to afford the option of the penitent's kneeling at the fixed confessional grill in the usual way [so that] in every case the freedom of the penitent is . . . respected."[24]

Environment and Art in Catholic Worship highlights the use of the word "chapel" to designate the place of reconciliation: "The word 'chapel' more appropriately describes this space."[25]

This same document advises that "a room or rooms for the reconciliation of individual penitents may be located near the baptismal area (when that is at the entrance) or in another convenient place."[26] The choice to locate the reconciliation chapel near the baptismal area is one which demonstrates the connection between the forgiveness of sins in baptism and God's repeated forgiveness in the sacrament of penance.

The "furnishings and decoration" of the room "should be simple and austere, offering the penitent a choice between face-to-face encounter or the anonymity provided by a screen, with nothing superfluous in evidence beyond a simple cross, table and bible."[27] This is recommended so that the true purpose of the room is immediately realized. "The purpose of this room is primarily for the celebration of the reconciliation liturgy; it is not a lounge, counseling room, etc."[28]

The place of reconciliation should be a chapel, which is reserved for this sacrament. It should not double as a vesting room, a storage room, a closet, or a part-time sacristy. Its furnishings should be simple and clearly state the purpose of the room. Options should be provided to the penitent for face-to-face confession or the use of a screen. In either case, the penitent should also be able to choose to sit or to kneel. As many options as possible should be provided to the penitent, since this chapel is the usual place for celebration of the sacrament of penance. "Confessions are not to be heard outside the confessional without a just cause,"[29] states the Code of Canon Law.

Conclusion

In general, the reverence shown to the reconciliation chapel flows from the theology of sin and penance found in the documents of the Church. The theology of reconciliation should inform praxis, which includes anything connected with the liturgy of reconciliation. "The assembly's celebration, that is, celebration in the midst of the faith community, by the whole community, is the normal and normative way of celebrating any sacrament or other liturgy."[30] Even when this communal dimension is not apparent, as in the celebration of the sacrament of penance, "the clergy or minister functions within the context of the entire community."[31] The Christian's purpose exists in participating in worship through celebrations of the sacrament of penance in a chapel set aside for this purpose.

Notes

1. BB, no. 1203.
2. RP, no. 8.
3. Ibid.
4. Ibid., no. 9.
5. Ibid., no. 11.
6. BB, no. 1150.
7. RP, no. 5.
8. Ibid.
9. Ibid.
10. Ibid., no. 6.
11. Ibid., no. 46.
12. Ibid., no. 18.
13. BB, no. 1208.
14. Ibid., no. 1212.
15. Ibid.
16. Ibid.
17. Ibid.
18. Ibid.
19. Ibid., no. 1213.
20. RP, no. 12.
21. CCL, 964:1.
22. Ibid., 964:2.
23. BCLN 12 (December 1974) n.p.
24. Ibid.
25. EACW, no. 81.
26. Ibid.
27. Ibid.
28. Ibid.
29. CCL, 964:3.
30. EACW, no. 31.
31. Ibid.

Bibliography

Bishops' Committee on the Liturgy Newsletter. Washington: National Conference of Catholic Bishops, 1965–90.

Book of Blessings. New York: Catholic Book Publishing Co., 1989.

Calabuig, Ignazio M. *The Dedication of a Church and an Altar: A Theological Commentary*. Washington: United States Catholic Conference, 1980.

Coriden, James A., Thomas J. Green, and Donald E. Heintschel, eds. *The Code of Canon Law: A Text and Commentary*. New York: Paulist, 1985.

Dedication of a Church and an Altar. Washington: United States Catholic Conference, 1978.

Environment and Art in Catholic Worship. Washington: United States Catholic Conference, 1978.

Flannery, Austin, ed. *Vatican Council II: The Conciliar and Post Conciliar Documents*. (Study Edition.) Northport, N.Y.: Costello, 1975 and 1986.

General Instruction of the Roman Missal. Liturgy Documentary Series: 2. Washington: United States Catholic Conference, 1982.

"Holy Communion and Worship of the Eucharist Outside of Mass." Vol. I: *Holy Communion Outside of Mass*. Vol. II: *Administration of Communion and Viaticum to the Sick by an Extraordinary Minister*. Vol. III: *Forms of Worship of the Eucharist: Exposition, Benediction, Processions, Congresses*. Washington: United States Catholic Conference, 1976.

Lectionary for Mass: Introduction. Liturgy Documentary Series 1. Washington: United States Catholic Conference, 1982.

Melloh, John Allyn. "The Rite of Dedication." *Assembly* 10, no. 2 (November 1983) 232.

Music in Catholic Worship, rev. ed. Washington: United States Catholic Conference, 1983.

Order of Christian Funerals. Collegeville: The Liturgical Press, 1989.

Pastoral Care of the Sick: Rites of Anointing and Viaticum. Collegeville: The Liturgical Press, 1983.

"Preparing and Celebrating the Paschal Feasts." Circular Letter from the Congregation for Divine Worship, January 16, 1988. *Origins* 17, no. 40. Washington: National Catholic News Service (March 1988).

"Rite for the Dedication of a Church: A Commentary." *Newsletter: International Commission on English in the Liturgy* 4, no. 4 (October–December 1977) 3.

Rite of Baptism for Children. Collegeville: The Liturgical Press, 1970.

Rite of Christian Initiation of Adults. Washington: United States Catholic Conference, 1988.

The Rite of Penance. Collegeville: The Liturgical Press, 1975.

The Roman Pontifical I. "Ordination of Priests." "Ordination of a Bishop." Vatican City: Vatican Polyglot Press, 1978.

The Sacramentary. New York: Catholic Book Publishing Co., 1985.

This Holy and Living Sacrifice: Directory for the Celebration and Reception of Communion Under Both Kinds. Washington: United States Catholic Conference, 1985.